Cambridge Elements

Elements in Global Philosophy of Religion
edited by
Yujin Nagasawa
University of Oklahoma

CONTEMPORARY PAGAN PHILOSOPHY

Eric Steinhart
William Paterson University

CAMBRIDGE
UNIVERSITY PRESS

Shaftesbury Road, Cambridge CB2 8EA, United Kingdom

One Liberty Plaza, 20th Floor, New York, NY 10006, USA

477 Williamstown Road, Port Melbourne, VIC 3207, Australia

314–321, 3rd Floor, Plot 3, Splendor Forum, Jasola District Centre,
New Delhi – 110025, India

103 Penang Road, #05–06/07, Visioncrest Commercial, Singapore 238467

Cambridge University Press is part of Cambridge University Press & Assessment,
a department of the University of Cambridge.

We share the University's mission to contribute to society through the pursuit of education, learning and research at the highest international levels of excellence.

www.cambridge.org
Information on this title: www.cambridge.org/9781009452359

DOI: 10.1017/9781009452373

When citing this work, please include a reference to the DOI 10.1017/9781009452373

First published 2024

A catalogue record for this publication is available from the British Library

ISBN 978-1-009-45235-9 Hardback
ISBN 978-1-009-45238-0 Paperback
ISSN 2976-5749 (online)
ISSN 2976-5730 (print)

Contemporary Pagan Philosophy

Elements in Global Philosophy of Religion

DOI: 10.1017/9781009452373
First published online: December 2024

Eric Steinhart
William Paterson University

Author for correspondence: Eric Steinhart, steinharte@wpunj.edu

Abstract: One of the most remarkable features of the current religious landscape in the West is the emergence of new Pagan religions. Here the author will use techniques from recent analytic philosophy of religion to try to clarify and understand the major themes in contemporary Paganisms. They will discuss Pagan concepts of nature, looking at nature as a network of animated agents. They will examine several Pagan theologies, and Pagan ways of relating to deities, such as theurgy. They will discuss Pagan practices like divination, visualization, and magic. And they will talk about Pagan ethics. Their discussions are based on extensive references to contemporary Pagan writings, from many different traditions. New Pagan religions, and new Pagan philosophies, have much to contribute to the religious future of the West, and to contemporary analytic philosophy of religion.

Keywords: Paganism, animism, theology, magic, rituals

ISBNs: 9781009452359 (HB), 9781009452380 (PB), 9781009452373 (OC)
ISSNs: 2976-5749 (online), 2976-5730 (print)

Contents

1 Paganisms Old and New

One of the most remarkable features of the current religious landscape in the West is the emergence of new Pagan religions. To put it generally, *Pagan* religions are animistic and polytheistic; they tend to view nature as a network of reciprocally interacting agents, some of which are divine partners in our religious activities (see York, 2003: ch. 3). However, since this Element needs to be very short, I will have to focus on a small set of specific religions within this general definition. I will therefore focus on the generally Pagan religions rooted in the indigenous cultures of Europe or the Mediterranean basin. A *contemporary Pagan* religion (also called a *Neopagan* religion) is any modern religious movement that takes itself to be reviving ancient Pagan religiosity.[1]

Paganism has a long history in the West (Myers, 2013). But modern Paganism, because it's young, is changing very rapidly. All I can do here is to outline some of the main philosophical themes in some of the more well-developed Pagan movements. Following many others (e.g. Davy, 2007: 5; Pizza & Lewis, 2009: 1; Rountree, 2010: 6–7; Hedenborg-White, 2014: 316; see Horak, 2020: 129–130), I will proceed by the *way of example*. And while I will mention some historical or sociological information in this introduction, I will quickly shift to philosophy, focusing on existence and value.

Druidry. Probably the earliest Neopagan religion is modern *Druidry* (or Druidism), which emerged in the late 1700s in Britain. Although these modern Druids took themselves to be reviving the ancient indigenous religions of the British Isles, they were mostly creating a new religion. Druidry focuses on the powers flowing through the natural world, and it looks a lot like a non-Christian kind of religious naturalism.

Wicca. Wicca is probably the largest Neopagan religion (White, 2015). It was mainly invented by Gerald Gardner in the 1930s and 1940s (Hutton, 2019). Wicca includes many ancient Pagan ideas and practices. Gardner cites many ancient Neoplatonic texts.[2] Those texts talk about themes later emphasized in Wicca, such as visualization, astrology, divination, magic, theurgy, polytheism, and reincarnation. Theologically, Wicca posits an original Source, which is

[1] Occult and esoteric organizations (e.g. Thelema, Ordo Templi Orientis, the Golden Dawn, Theosophy) contributed to early Neopaganism. However, they are highly dependent on Christianity and Judaism, and are therefore excluded from Paganism here. Likewise, Satanism and New Age spirituality are not Pagan.

[2] Gardner (1954: 159) cites the Neoplatonic text *On the Mysteries*, by Iamblichus. He also cites (1954: 92; 1959: 108) the *Platonic Theology* by Proclus. Gardner (1959: 171–174) extensively discusses the Neoplatonic text *On the Gods and the World*, by Sallustius, who was inspired by Iamblichus.

often explicitly identified with the Neoplatonic One. The One produces a Goddess and a God. Wiccans often say our universe is animated by divine energies, which we can arouse in our bodies to work magic.

Witchcraft. Contemporary witchcraft emerges from Wicca, but drops its initiatory and ceremonial aspects, and often drops Wiccan theology. It keeps the basic structure of Wiccan magic.

Asatru. The old Norse-Germanic religions involved deities like Odin and Freya, and their revivals began in Germany in the late 1800s. Today these Neopagan revivals are known as *Heathen* religions, and the most widely practiced form of Heathenry is *Asatru*. Asatru is closely based on the Norse mythologies surviving in the *Prose Edda* and *Poetic Edda* (the *lore*). The lore was probably first recorded in the 1200s. Asatruars use the lore to inspire their theologies, ethics, and religious practices. Asatru tends towards animism. It includes public and private religious rituals. Some Asatruars practice Norse shamanism (*seidr*) or magic using runes and other objects.

Hellenism. Hellenism revives the ritual practices of the ancient Greeks, and mainly starts in the 1990s. Hellenists take inspiration from classical texts, as well as from the Medieval philosopher Plethon. *Neoplatonic reconstructionists* are reviving Neoplatonism independently of any Greek ethnicity. Hellenists and Neoplatonists venerate the Olympian deities; they practice magic, theurgy, astrology, and so on. The new Stoics are reviving and modernizing ancient Roman practices, and they deserve to be classified as Neopagan. However, since fine books already exist on the new Stoicisms (e.g. Pigliucci, 2017), I will not discuss them here. Other ethnic Neopaganisms exist in Europe, such as Baltic and Slavic Paganisms (Aitamurto & Simpson, 2014; Rountree, 2015). But space constraints prevent me from dealing with these "native faith" movements here.

Following this list, I will focus on Druidry, Wicca, witchcraft, Asatru, Hellenism, and Neoplatonic revivalism. Many people build *eclectic Paganisms* by combining elements from these traditions. I am painfully aware that this list is incomplete, but, again, my space is severely limited. Space likewise forces me to omit topics like neo-shamanism (and its uses of entheogens), and I mostly omit the ceremonial aspects of Paganism.[3] Here I will be doing *analytic philosophy of Neopagan religion*.[4] I read lots of Pagan texts, both ancient and modern; I find some common themes; I try to use techniques from recent analytic philosophy to clarify and explain those themes. I intend neither to endorse nor to criticize Neopaganisms; I merely aim to understand them philosophically.

---

[3] For ceremony, see Meredith (2013) and Steinhart (2016).

[4] Myers (2013) and Kadmus (2018) do non-analytic philosophy of paganism.

When I do this analytic work, I will use various theories from recent analytic metaphysics. Although all these theories are well-defended, they remain controversial. Importantly, I do not claim that they are true; I claim only that they are useful in understanding Pagan themes. For example, I will use both realism about causal powers and realism about possible worlds (modal realism), as well as branching space-times, and backwards causation. Again, I do not claim that these theories are true; here I'm merely applying them. Moreover, I lack the space to discuss these theories in any depth. I will mention a few landmark texts, but this is not the place for background studies.

When I do this analytic work, I'm using many Pagan texts to motivate my analyses. However, contemporary Paganisms have no holy scriptures, no standard doctrines, and no centralized authorities. So, while I try to use texts that are generally well-regarded, they are not orthodox in any sense. And these Pagan religions are so diverse that anything anybody says about them is easily contradicted. At best, I am making vague, approximate, and partial generalizations. But Pagans regard this diversity as a virtue. Consequently, I must stress again that I'm not outlining any official positions. The philosophy of Neopaganism is in its infancy, and here I am only taking awkward baby steps.

2 Nature as Energized Network

2.1 The Watery Abyss

According to the old Egyptian mythology from Heliopolis, all things emerged from a primordial nothingness. It was personified as the deity Nun and symbolized as a watery abyss (Van Dijk, 1995; Fiala, 2008; Bernabe, 2020). In the Greek myths, Homer portrays all things as emerging from a watery abyss (*Illiad* 14.246). The abyss appears in Norse myths. In the *Voluspa* story in the *Poetic Edda*, the Seeress declares that, in the beginning, there was only an abyss: "no sand nor sea nor cool waves; earth was nowhere nor the sky above, [only] a void of yawning chaos (*gap var ginnunga*)" (Larrington, 2014: 4). This abyss (now called *Ginnungagap*) occurs again in the *Gylfaginning* creation story in the *Prose Edda*. Here the abyss has ice on the one side and fire on the other, and these polarities interact to form liquid water in the middle of the abyss.

Philosophers have traditionally offered conceptual interpretations of myths. Since I'm writing here as a philosopher, it's my job to interpret these (and other) Pagan myths. On my interpretation, these myths point to an *original nothingness*, symbolized as a watery abyss. All that exists emerges from that great void. Of course, since this abyss is truly original, its originality is logical rather than temporal; it is not the first moment of time. And its emptiness is logical rather than spatial: it is neither empty space, nor the empty world, nor the empty set.

For modern exactness, I'll follow Oliver and Smiley (2013), and say nothingness is the *x* such that *x* is not identical with *x*. This nothingness does not exist; it is *absolute nonexistence*. Since even Pagans have to explain why there is something rather than nothing, nothingness is the right place to start.

Nothingness and existence are linked by *negation*. Tillich says: "one can describe being in terms of non-non-being; . . . One could say that 'being is the negation of the primordial night of nothingness'" (1952: 40). But how does this negation occur? One answer looks like this: nothingness is non-being, and if non-being negates itself, then its self-negation is non-non-being, that is, being (Priest, 2001: 244; Priest, 2014: 180, fn. 34).[5] A good ancient Pagan symbol for this self-negating nothingness is the *Ouroboros*, the serpent with its tail in its mouth. Its self-eating symbolizes its self-negation. The Ouroboros appears in Egyptian and Greek myths. It appears as the Norse world-serpent *Midgardsormr*, which surrounds the earth, holding its tail in its mouth.

More precisely, Steinhart argues that being-itself is the self-negation of non-being (2020a: sec. 6.1.3; 2022: ch. 2). His *Argument for Being-Itself* goes like this: (1) Nothingness is absolutely negative. (2) Since its negativity is absolute, its negativity is universal; since its negativity is universal, it negates itself. (3) Just as nothingness is not the nonexistence of this or that being, so its self-negation is not the existence of this or that being. Rather, the self-negation of nothingness is *being-itself*. But this self-negation does not create being-itself; on the contrary, it is *identical* with being-itself.

2.2 Pagan Protology

Our Ouroboros, having bitten its own tail, is the first existing entity. Ouroboros is closely linked with the Egyptian deity Atum. Atum is the primordial mound of earth, which rose up out of the watery abyss Nun (Van Dijk, 1995: 1699–1700). On my philosophical interpretation, Atum symbolizes being-itself. Something similar occurs in Norse myths, in which the waters in the abyss self-organize into the primal being Ymir. Ymir is closely associated with the emergence of earth (*Voluspa*, verses 3 & 4; *Vafthurdnir*, verse 21; *Gylfaginning*). Of course, Ymir is not Atum. But their conceptual similarities motivate the philosophical thesis that some primal being emerges from the abyss.

The primal being Atum combines male and female sexual powers and, through self-fertilization, generates the world. According to the Greek poet Hesiod, the primal being is Chaos, and Chaos produces in various sexual ways

[5] This answer probably originates with Boehme (*Mysterium Pansophicum*, 1.1–2.1); it appears in Peirce (1965: 1.175, 1.409, 6.33, 6.214–219, 6.612, 8.317); and in Heidegger (1929).

the earth, sky, oceans, and so on (*Theogeny*, 115–134). According to the Pythagoreans, the primal being is *the One*. For them, the One is chaos and darkness; it dwells in the earth like a hermaphroditic seed, which has both male and female sexual powers (Pseudo-Iamblichus, *Theology of Arithmetic,* 4–5). Likewise, in the Norse myths, Ymir is hermaphroditic. And the body of Ymir gets chopped up to make the earth, sky, oceans, and so on. The similarities between Atum, Chaos, the Pythagorean One, and Ymir suggest that, even if they are not identical, they are compatible. They motivate the philosophical thesis that the primal being has both male and female powers, which sexually unite to generate the world.

Scholars have traced a somewhat sketchy path from Atum, through the sun-god Aten, to the Platonic One (Flegel, 2018; DeConick, 2020). Whatever its exact origins might have been, the One becomes central to Greco-Roman *protology*, the study of origins. The Platonic One was developed by late Roman Pagans like Plotinus, Iamblichus, Sallustius, and Proclus. They defined the One as the all-powerful source of the existence of all the beings among beings.[6] But the One is not any such being; on the contrary, the One is being-itself. The One escapes from all descriptions (it is ineffable, or beyond predication). The best explanation for this escape is that the One is pure *wildness*.

Something like the Platonic One appears in many Neopagan protologies. Neoplatonic reconstructionists talk about it (MacLennan, 2013; Butler, 2014; Williams, 2016; Opsopaus, 2022). Since Hellenic polytheism has roots in ancient Neoplatonism, some Hellenists discuss it (Alexander, 2007).[7] The One appears in Wicca. Gardner cites Iamblichus, Sallustius, and Proclus (1954: 92, 159; 1959: 108, 171–174). Many Wiccans refer to the One, or refer to it as the "Source" or "Ultimate Deity" (e.g., Farrar & Farrar, 1981: 49, 154; Buckland, 1986: 19; Cantrell, 2001: 24; Cunningham, 2004: 123; Silver Elder, 2011: 9, 18; Cuhulain, 2011: 14). For Starhawk, the One is the ground of being, the ground of being is the Goddess, and the Goddess floats "in the abyss of outer darkness" (1999: 131, 48, 121, 41). Those versions of witchcraft that come from Wicca often assume a deep Source of energy for working magic, and their Source resembles the One.

Something like the One appears in Druidry. Greer says that "every being in the whole universe is a unique individual expression of the One Life" (2021: 53). The

---

[6] Ancient Neoplatonists often described the One as transcendent. Since Neopagans often object to transcendence, they might reject that One. However, Plotinus also places the One in the earth as a root (*Enneads* 3.3.7, 3.8.10, 6.8.15), as a seed (4.8.6.1–10), or as a spring (3.8.10.1–5, 5.2.1, 5.7.12.23–7). This One-in-the-earth resembles the Neopagan One.

[7] The governing body of Greek Hellenic polytheism endorses the One ("En"). See www.ysee.gr/faq-eng.html, accessed June 21, 2023.

One Life manifests or expresses itself in different ways in all things (48–50). Greer equates the One Life with the Stoic *pneuma*, the energetic breath that animates all things (47). The One Life is his translation of the old Welsh term *nwyfre*. Greer says all things are "woven together into a unity by the flowing currents of *nwyfre*" (48). And Billington says that for Druids *nwyfre* is the "living, energising current of life that flows through all living beings" (2011: 11). Byghan uses the Irish word *anam* to refer to this universal life force (2018: 6). The One Life is a universal energy that manifests all things and unifies all things; but these are also crucial features of the One. More generally, Greer argues that Neopagans would greatly benefit from a revival of Neoplatonic protology (2019).

But what about Asatru? On the one hand, there are some affinities between the chaotic and hermaphroditic Pythagorean One and the Norse primal being Ymir. On the other hand, the Platonic One, which becomes assimilated to the Good and the sun, seems entirely alien to Norse-Germanic Paganism. Asatruars often endorse animism (Lafayllve, 2013: 10; Nordvig, 2020: 36; Paxson, 2021: 149), and animism typically requires some kind of deep power or energy. Moreover, it's plausible that Asatru makes philosophical sense; if it does, then it has some protology. And it's plausible that Asatru overlaps with other Pagan protologies. It is therefore reasonable to think that the protologies of all the Paganisms on our list share a *minimal common core:* some primal being exists; the primal being is being-itself; being-itself is absolute creative power; this power is conceptualized in terms of natural polarities like fire-ice, male-female, and so on. This common core evolves in one way in the Greco-Roman Paganisms (as the One that radiates power). It evolves differently in the Norse-Germanic Paganisms (as creative natural power itself).

2.3 Isness Is Energy

Here I will use the neutral term *Isness* to refer to the common core of all our Pagan protologies. Isness is that which all beings have in common; it is being-itself. Isness is that which manifests or expresses itself in all things, which weaves all things together into a unified network and which animates all things and gives them agency. Perhaps Isness is emanated by the One; perhaps Isness just exists fundamentally. The fundamental Pagan principle is that *being is power;* to be is to act on and to be acted on.

Many Pagans use the term *energy* to refer to Isness. The term *energy* is by far the most common conceptual term in all the Paganisms in our list. Pagans tend to use "energy" differently than physicists. Pagan energy is *strength of propensity for action*. Consider acids, which are ordered from weak to strong. Stronger acids have greater propensities to perform the characteristic actions of acids, that is, to exercise the causal powers of acids. Stronger acids have greater energies. Likewise, stronger magnets have greater propensities to generate electrical currents, to attract metals, and so on. Stronger magnets have greater energies. Energy is strength for manifestation; it is the strength with which some power appears or makes itself present to other powers with greater effects.

Some Pagans link energy directly to the One. Plotinus often says that the One is absolutely infinite power (*Enneads*, 2.4.15, 5.5.10, 6.7.32, 6.9.6, etc.). It is the power that makes beings be (*Enneads*, 5.1.6). Starhawk says, "The world of separate things is the reflection of the One; the One is the reflection of the myriad separate things of the world. We are all 'swirls' of the same energy, yet each swirl is unique in its own form and pattern" (1999: 49). Crowley says, "the Divine is energy" and "the Divine is seen as ultimately One" (2003: 1). For Druids, the universal energy is the One Life (Carr-Gomm, 2006: 55; Greer, 2021: 47–53). Every thing is an expression of the One Life, which is the power that animates all things and which flows between all things.

Other Pagans link energy to networks. Alexander says Pagans "see the world as surrounded by an energetic matrix that connects everything to everything else. This matrix, or 'cosmic web,' envelops our earth . . . and extends throughout the solar system and beyond. The web pulses with subtle vibrations" (2014: 48). Sebastiani says, "all things contain and are made of energy" (2020: 8). Starhawk says, "the universe is a fluid, ever-changing energy pattern, not a collection of fixed and separate things" (1999: 155). Energy is central in many witchcraft and Wiccan books (Stein, 1990; Starhawk, 1999; Alexander, 2014; Murphy-Hiscock, 2017; Squire, 2021). Thus Wiccans say, "all things are manifestations of an underlying energy or spiritual force" (Roderick, 2005: 2).

This Pagan protology entails that *Isness is absolute power:* (1) Since non-being is absolute, its negation is also absolute. (2) Nothingness is absolute *powerlessness*, but the absolute self-negation of absolute powerlessness is absolute power. (3) Since the self-negation of non-being is Isness, Isness is absolute power. However, Isness is not an absolutely powerful being; on the contrary, since Isness is being-itself, Isness is not any being at all. Isness is just identical with its absolute power; it is energy-itself. Isness is the power that drives every existing thing to exercise its causal powers. It is the energy that expresses itself in that being. This protology also entails that *Isness is absolute positivity:* (1) Nothingness is absolute negativity. (2) But the absolute self-negation of absolute negativity is absolute positivity. (3) Since the self-negation of non-being is Isness, Isness is absolute positivity. Isness is absolutely positive energy. Analogously, since nothingness is absolutely unproductive, Isness is absolutely productive energy.

2.4 Networks

As the ground of being, Isness is not any existing thing. According to Filler (2019), the One (Isness) is *pure relationality*. Pagans stress that everything is related (or connected) to everything (Beckett, 2017: 195). Sebastiani affirms that for the Pagan "all things are bound and connected" (2020: 8, 52). Wildermuth says Pagans see "everything as mutual relation and obligation" (2021: 101). Greer says, "Since humans, gods, and all other beings inhabit a common world and share in a network of reciprocal relationships of exchange, every being is connected to every other being in a closely woven fabric of reciprocity" (2023: 102). Wiccans and witches affirm that all things are connected (Alexander, 2014: 35, 48–50; Batty, 2023: 145–146). Druids affirm it (Carr-Gomm, 2006: 37–45; Byghan, 2018: 6; Greer, 2021: 48). Asatruars do too (Lafayllve, 2013: 146; Paxson, 2021: 135–137). This connection involves shared energy. Greer says everything is "woven together into a unity by the flowing currents" of the One Life (2021: 48). As a Druid, you should "Think of every atom around you as being held in place by a lattice of life force" (2021: 48). Starhawk tells us that "All is interwoven into the continuous fabric of being. Its warp and weft are energy" (1999: 155). Starhawk starts with polarity and generalizes it to define reality as a *network* in which every point is connected to every point:

> Polarity . . . is a net of forces between a multiplicity of nodes in a sphere . . . draw two points and connect them with a straight line. Picture it as a line of reverberating force flowing both backward and forward at once, and you can well imagine how power can be generated. Now draw a larger circle and mark a number of points. . . . Now connect them with lines in every way you can. (1999: 234)

Pagans tend to refer to the network of beings as *Nature*. The view that Nature is a network has an important place in current analytic metaphysics (Dipert, 1997; Ladyman, 2023). Both analytic thinkers and Neopagans will benefit by combining their ideas. It's important to stress that *Nature is all-inclusive*. Nature includes everything on earth. Humans and all their technologies are entirely natural. Nature includes everything in our universe. Nature is not restricted to our universe, nor to some quantum-mechanical multiverse based on our universe. Modal realism posits a plenitude of other concrete possible worlds (Lewis, 1986). If that is true, then Nature includes all those worlds. Nature is the All. On this Pagan theory of Nature, there are no extra-natural or supernatural beings.

Our protology says that Isness is both absolutely productive power and pure relationality. It therefore generates an all-inclusive network (Nature) in which every node connects to every node. However, since Isness is not any thing among things, Isness is not identical with this network. Rather, Isness is the *existence* of the network. Even more precisely, Isness is the existence of every node and every relation in the network. It is the *being* of every part of the network (and every whole is a part of itself). But if Isness were divided up and distributed bit by bit to different parts of the network, then it would not be unified, so Isness would not be Isness. Hence it is not chopped up and parceled out, but rather Isness is *wholly present* in every part of the network.[8] Plotinus refers to this as the *integral omnipresence* of Isness (*Enneads*, 6.4–5). Isness is *immanent* in the network. It does *not* transcend the network; it is not outside of or beyond the network. Likewise, nothingness, which does not exist at all, is not outside of or beyond Nature.

Isness manifests Nature.[9] Thus Nature is that network of beings whose existence is Isness. Isness is absolutely powerful positivity, and I'll refer to that powerful positivity as *greatness*. This greatness is the greatest greatness, which integrates every other greatness into a unity. It's maximal greatness. So, Nature is that network of beings whose existence is maximal greatness. But if the existence of any network is maximal greatness, then that network is the maximally greatest network. Consequently, Nature is that network than which no greater is possible. Here *possibility* is used in the widest sense, as consistent definability: every consistently definable entity is part of Nature. Iamblichus and Proclus seem to argue for many maximally perfect gods. But an absolutely infinite whole contains absolutely infinitely many absolutely infinite parts (Plotinus, *Enneads*, 6.7.15.25–30). Hence Nature can contain absolutely infinitely many maximally perfect gods. Nature is *indefinitely extensible* (in the mathematical sense): if any definition of Nature allows some greater being to be added to Nature to make something apparently greater than Nature, then that original definition of Nature merely defined a proper part of Nature, and Nature as a whole already contains that greater being.[10] Cicero thought of Nature as that than which no greater is possible (*On the Nature of the Gods,* II.18–47). He used that greatness to argue for various features of Nature, and here I follow his method.

8 Isness exists in Hypatia, but the-Isness-in-Hypatia is not Hypatia. Likewise the-Isness-in-Socrates is not Socrates. Since the Isness in these different humans is qualified by its differences, the-Isness-in-Hypatia is not identical with the-Isness-in-Socrates. But the Isness in the-Isness-in-Hypatia is identical with the Isness in the-Isness-in-Socrates.

9 For those Pagans who affirm the One, the One emanates Isness, which manifests Nature.

10 Hence Nature satisfies mathematical reflection principles.

2.5 The Surpassivity of Nature

According to this Pagan theory, Nature is a maximally great network. If Nature does not contain absolutely infinitely many nodes, then Nature does not contain the greatest number of beings, but then Nature is not maximally great; therefore, since Nature is maximally great, Nature does contain absolutely infinitely many nodes.[11] And if the nodes are not universally connected (each connected to itself and to every other), then Nature does not contain the greatest system of connections; but then Nature is not maximally great; therefore, since Nature is maximally great, its nodes are universally connected.

A *universe* is any maximal physical whole, meaning that it is closed system of spatial, temporal, and causal relations.[12] Nature contains our universe and all the networks in our universe. Our universe contains networks at every scale. Its space-time is a network of regions.[13] Perhaps it contains a network of entangled quantum bits of information (Wen, 2018). It does contain networks of particles, atoms, molecules, organisms, and so on. Our universe may (or may not) be infinitely large; however, since it is not absolutely infinitely large, it is just a proper part of Nature. Nature is greater than our universe.

Since universes are open to variation in their spatio-temporal structures, and in their causal powers, and since the variation of any relational structure just produces another relational structure, Nature contains the greatest consistently definable system of universes. These universes are all possible with respect to each other. Hence this theory of Nature supports the *modal realism* of Lewis (1986), which argues for a plurality of possible worlds (I refer to his "worlds" as universes). A universe is *actual* for all the things in it, while the others are *non-actual* for them. Suppose we live in universe Arda, while Thor lives in universe Asgard. Then Arda is actual for us, but non-actual for Thor, while Asgard is actual for Thor but non-actual for us. The class of possible universes may be infinitely large; however, since it is not absolutely infinitely large, Nature exceeds it.

The greatness of Nature entails that it contains every consistently definable structure. Hence a principle of plenitude, which states that consistency entails existence, holds in Nature (see Balaguer, 1998). Nature contains every consistently definable mathematical structure (such as every model of every consistently definable set theory). To adopt a phrase from Hartshorne (1965: 28–32), *Nature*

[11] Absolutely infinite structures resemble proper classes in mathematics.

[12] Causal relations are interactions between causal powers and their manifestation partners. A causal power in one universe does not interact with any manifestation partners in some other universe.

[13] A region is a set of space-time points; a space-time point is a tuple of numbers. Some philosophers may say that numbers, tuples, and sets are abstract; hence regions are abstract. If they also want to say that regions are concrete, they will have to say that some abstract objects are concrete. I avoid any abstract/concrete dualism.

is the self-surpassing surpasser of all. Nature transcends itself because Isness is wholly present in every part of Nature. Since Nature is *self-transcendent*, Nature is *ineffable.*

Pagans often talk about a structure known as the *world tree*. Plotinus often talks about the world tree (*Enneads*, 3.3.7, 3.8.10, 4.4.1, 4.4.11, 4.8.6, 6.8.15). He uses it to illustrate the unfolding of the One into multiplicity. Some Wiccans and witches use world trees, aka the tree of life (e.g. Starhawk, 1999: 68; Sabin, 2011: 16–17; Murphy-Hiscock, 2017: 39). Trees are religiously central in Druidry. The world tree appears as Yggdrasil in Norse cosmology and in modern Asatru (Andren, 2014; Paxson, 2021: 134–137). The world tree appears in the evolutionary tree of life, unfolding from the first living thing to the many forms of life today. In pure mathematics, the axioms of set theory have models that resemble trees. These purely mathematical trees are also world trees, and they are parts of Nature. Thus world trees occur in many ways in Nature.

2.6 The Positivities of Nature

The greatness of Nature includes more than just physical or mathematical structures. It includes the greatest system of mutually compatible positivities. These are properties like *containing the maximal degrees of all positive properties*. So greatness defines a network that contains maximal power (energy), complexity, diversity, beauty, vitality, intelligence, justice, virtue, and so on. Moreover, the network itself transcends all its positivities; while it contains maximal beauty, the network itself transcends beauty.[14] So, if Nature does not include the maximal degrees of all positive properties, then it is not maximally great. However, since Nature is maximally great, Nature contains the maximal degrees of all positive properties. Nature contains maximal power (energy), complexity, diversity, beauty, vitality, intelligence, justice, virtue, and so on.

From the thesis that Nature contains maximal positivity, it does not follow that every part of nature is maximally positive. From the fact that our universe (for example) contains some brightest star, it does not follow that every star is maximally bright. Pagans affirm that the positivities within Nature interact in both cooperative and competitive ways. Due to these interactions, many parts of Nature are simple, monotonous, ugly, lifeless, unintelligent, unjust, vicious, evil, and so on. For example, on earth, evolution by natural selection entails that organisms compete and conflict with each other. Animals kill and eat other animals. But that struggle for life drives the evolution of functional excellence (what the Greeks

[14] Just as the proper class of ordinals contains all ordinals but is not itself an ordinal (on pain of contradiction), so the network contains all beauty but is not itself beautiful. Just as the proper class of sets transcends setness (and so is not a set), so the network transcends all its positivities.

called *arete*, which emerges through the strife in the *agon*, that is, through conflict). The most extreme forms of conflict (the evolutionary arms races between predators and prey, parasites and hosts, and so on) drive the emergence of some of the most extreme positivities of organisms. Gazelles and cheetahs are glorious, and they evolved their biological virtues (speed, strength, agility) through their conflict.

Axiology is the study of value, and modern Pagans can adopt four axiological points from Plotinus. First, Plotinus argued that evils emerge from conflicts among the goods of the parts of Nature (*Enneads*, 3.2.2–4; 3.2.15–17; 4.4.32; 4.4.39.23–30; 6.6.1–3, etc.). Second, Plotinus argued that the conflicts among the parts are integrated into the greater complexity, harmony, and beauty of the whole (*Enneads*, 2.3.16–18, 3.2.11, 3.2.16–17, 3.3.1, etc.). Third, Isness drives every thing to surpass itself, and this universal self-surpassing transforms all local evils into greater goods (*Enneads*, 3.2.5, 3.2.15–18). Fourth, while evil exists in the conflicts among parts, the whole of Nature is good (*Enneads*, 3.2.3, 3.2.11, 3.2.17, 4.4.32). And the whole of Nature is absolutely infinitely rich. Our universe is an infinitesimally small part of Nature, and humanity is an insignificantly small part of our universe. Nature does not exist for us. No argument runs from the absolutely powerful positivity of Isness to the maximization of human happiness.

Pagans often say that Nature is worthy of reverence (Carr-Gomm, 2006: 37; Beckett, 2017: ch. 3; Murphy-Hiscock, 2017: 14; Sebastiani, 2020: 4, 51; Paxson, 2021: 153; Wildermuth, 2021: 9–10; Batty, 2023: 47). Or that "holiness is in everything" (Paxson, 2021: *x*); or "Nature itself is sacred and holy" (Crowley, 2001: 7). Here is an argument: (1) Isness (being-itself) is the existence within every thing. Since this existence is not qualified by the things in which it exists, Isness is pure. But purity is holiness (Rogerson, 2003). Therefore, Isness is holy. (2) Nature as a whole is the perfect manifestation of being-itself. (3) Holiness passes through perfect manifestation: if something is holy, then whatever it perfectly manifests is holy too. (4) Therefore, Nature *as a whole* is holy. (5) But if something is holy, then it is worthy of reverence. So, Nature as a whole is worth of reverence. Since each thing in Nature exists, it logically contains Isness, as an immanent spark of holiness. Thus "holiness is in everything." Clearly, this does not entail that every part of Nature is holy; things have variable degrees of holiness.

3 Patterns of Energy

3.1 Animism

Animism is a common theme in Paganism today (Crowley, 2003: 179–180; Orr, 2011; Beckett, 2017: 57; Lupa, 2021: 57; Wildermuth, 2021: 12).[15] Wicca tends

[15] Another type of animism focuses on ethical and political obligations (Harvey, 2006). It is arguable that the major premise of this "New Animism" is that only persons deserve respect.

to endorse animism (Crowley, 2001: 21; Roderick, 2005: 2; Sabin, 2011: 25–27). Modern witchcraft emphasizes it (Alexander, 2014: 20, 59, 66; Murphy-Hiscock, 2017: 56; Sebastiani, 2020: 24). Druids affirm it (Carr-Gomm, 2006: 37; Billington, 2011: 5; Byghan, 2018: 6). Asatruars do too (Lafayllve, 2013: 10; Nordvig, 2020: 36; Paxson, 2021: 149–151).

The most common way Pagans define animism involves something called *Spirit*. On this definition, animism asserts that all things are animated by Spirit, so that every particular thing is animated by its own *spirit*. Obviously, to say things are animated by spirits does not imply that they are identical with spirits. Theories of Spirit now diverge. The *energy theory* of animism says that Spirit is some kind of power, and this is by far the most common Pagan theory of Spirit. The *vitality theory* elaborates the energy theory by adding biological features like vitality or life. The old words associated with Spirit, such as *pneuma*, *anima*, *anam*, *nwyfre*, and *spiritus* itself, tend to mean breath, and, therefore, life. The *mentality theory* extends the vitality theory by adding psychological features like intelligence, awakeness, self-consciousness, or personhood.

Since the energy theory is the core Pagan theory of animism, I will start with it (Steinhart, 2018). I will try to work out the Pagan thesis that things are animated by spirits, which are particular occurrences of Spirit. However, I will avoid words like *spirit* and *Spirit*. Those words have too much dualistic baggage, and I want to work out a nondualistic animism, which is based closely on current analytic metaphysics and philosophy of physics.[16] Contemporary Pagans often take ancient words (such as *wicca*, *nwyfre*, *orlog*, etc.) and give them new Pagan meanings, and here I will do the same. On the energy theory, Spirit is just Isness. And instead of a spirit, I will say an *eidolon*. Using these terms, animism asserts that things are generally animated by Isness, and each particular thing is animated by its own eidolon. Any eidolon is a specialization of Isness.

3.2 Eidolons Are Powerful Universals

The metaphysics in Section 2 entails that all things are energized, powered, or driven by the wildness of Isness. Isness is the deepest and most universal power of being, and is wholly present in every being. But the wildness of any thing (any node) in the network is bounded by its relations with other things. These bonds specialize the Isness in every thing, and any such specialization of Isness

But that thesis belongs clearly to Protestantism (e.g. Hobbes, Locke, Kant, etc.), and not to Paganism. The Pagan thesis of bounded sovereignty (and agency) entails that all things deserve respect whether or not they are persons. The "New Animism" is not dealt with here.

[16] Both mind/matter and abstract/concrete dualisms are rejected here.

is an eidolon. Since Isness is pure existential power, any specialization of Isness is a specialized power of being. Since Isness is maximally productive, every consistently definable eidolon exists in Nature. Each eidolon is a point in the Nature-network, linked to other eidolons, and to particular things, by many relations. Nature contains a system or world of eidolons.

According to the energy theory of animism, every particular thing is *animated* by its own eidolon, and any eidolon is a specialization of Isness. For example, in our universe, Isness specializes itself into the power of gravitational attraction, which is manifested by and only by things with the property of being massive, but that property is the eidolon *mass*. So the *property* of being massive (the eidolon mass) is correlated with the *power* of gravitational attraction. Perhaps this correlation is identity; perhaps it is something else. I will just say that *eidolons are powerful properties*. Since any specific power emerges from the relational specialization of Isness, any such power manifests itself when any instance of that power appears in appropriate relations with other powers.

Since Isness is the most general power to be, and eidolons are specializations of that power, every eidolon is the power to be in some specific way. Tillich writes that every particular tree "exists only because it participates in that power of being which is treehood, that power which makes every tree a tree" (1957: 21). But that power is the eidolon treehood (or treeness). Tillich says the form of a thing is "its *essentia*, its definite power of being" (1951: 178). Thus eidolons are *powerful essences* or *powerful forms*, here taken to include simple forms, and combinations of simpler forms into more complex forms.[17] As powerful essences or forms, eidolons are *powerful universals*. Things that resemble each other share universals. Since this oak resembles that oak, they share the universal oakness. Of course, particular oaks are highly variable. When any essence is instantiated, it is also instantiated with other eidolons, which are its variable accidents. Oakness is instantiated along with tallness here, and along with shortness over there.

The powers of eidolons are *causal powers*. From current analytic metaphysics, I adopt a version of *causal powers realism*.[18] On this version, causal powers are prior to global physical laws, which emerge from (or merely supervene on) the causal powers at space-time regions. If all the eidolons instantiated in some universe are identical (as in cellular automatons), then the laws that emerge over them may be exceptionless, unambiguous regularities. However, as universes grow more complex, and their ecologies of eidolons grow more diverse and variable, their global laws grow ever more probabilistic and ambiguous.

[17] Eidolons can be approximately modeled as algorithms (which may be transfinite).

[18] For causal powers realism, see Molnar (2006); Mumford & Anjum (2011); Ellis (2014); and Tugby (2022).

Complex universes are causally messy (Cartwright, 1999). Causal powers constrain each other. As universe grows more complex, those constraints become tangled up into tapestries filled with anomalies, irregularities, and exceptions. Yet those anomalies are not miracles, but follow naturally from the wild diversity of causal powers.

The eidolons order themselves according to their specificities: oakness is more specific than treeness, and treeness is more specific than plantness. The most specific eidolons are the particular forms, which are the forms of particular things. The form of Socrates (*Socratesness*) is the form of an individual body. If exact copies of Socrates exist, then Socratesness is equally shared by all those replicas too. Aristotle defines the *soul* as the most specific form of any living body with organs (*De Anima*, 412a5-414a33). So Socratesness (the form of his body) is the soul of Socrates. His soul is that power of being which makes Socrates be Socrates. Most Pagan animists generalize the concept of the soul so that all things have souls. My approach to animism affirms this generalization: every thing has a soul, which is its most specific eidolon.

Souls are causally powerful essences. Some souls include life, while others do not. Quarks have souls composed of only a few eidolons (mass, charge, strangeness, etc.). But quarks are not living organisms, and their souls do not include the eidolon life. On the other hand, bacteria are living things, and their souls include life, along with many other eidolons. Life includes eidolons like genetic codes, metabolism, reproduction, evolution, and so on. Some souls include mentality and personhood, while others do not. Quarks do not have minds, and are not persons, so their souls do not include mentality or personhood. On the other hand, many organisms (perhaps all organisms) do have minds, and so their souls include mentality. And humans, and probably many other animals, are persons. The souls of all humans, and those other animals, include the eidolon personhood.

Many Pagans endorse something like this eidetic animism. Orr writes that Spirit includes "those essential forces and energies that, moving within particular structures or patterns, vitalise and empower" (2011: 104). But that is Isness specializing itself into eidolons. Alexander says a spirit is "a unique energy pattern" (2014: 20). But spirits are just eidolons, which are unique energy patterns. The *nature spirits* defined by Lupa closely resemble universals or forms (2021: 22–23, 57). Nature spirits can be thought of as active universals (Crowley, 2003: 179–180; Murphy-Hiscock, 2017: 56). The souls of nymphs, fairies, elves, and so on are eidolons. Cicero thought many eidolons were divine (*On the Nature of the Gods,* II.71). For example, plantness is a divine eidolon which is sacred to Demeter. Plantness is part of the eidolon which animates

Demeter (the soul of Demeter). So her divine soul is instantiated in every whole composed of plants.

Eidolons form a system; they are related to each other, and to particular things, by many relations. So the system of eidolons is a *world*. Sometimes Pagans talk about a *spirit world* or Otherworld; if spirits are eidolons, this is the *eidolon world*. As patterns of power (Isness), eidolons resonate with each other. Alexander says, "Everything in the world emits an energy vibration of some kind. Different things have different energy patterns, resonances, or 'signatures.' These resonances reach out to touch one another in a series of criss-crossing lines all around the world" (2014: 48). As universals or forms, eidolons are not made of material particles; but they are not immaterial minds.

3.3 How Things Instantiate Eidolons

On the Pagan metaphysics of universes developed here, every universe has some space-time, which divides into a network of regions.[19] From current analytic metaphysics, I adopt *supersubstantivalism*, which says that universals *are instantiated at* space-time regions (Lehmkuhl, 2018; Duerr & Calosi, 2021).[20] An *instance* or *example* of a universal is a (universal, region) pair. Since eidolons are universals, eidolons are instantiated at space-time regions, and their instances are (eidolon, region) pairs. And, since eidolons are causally powerful, all the causal action in any universe emerges from the interactions among the causally powerful eidolons located at its regions.[21]

On this view, physical *things* are (eidolon, region) pairs. This oak tree is the pair (oakness, tree-shaped-region). Since eidolons are instantiated at regions, regions in turn instantiate their eidolons. The tree-shaped-region instantiates oakness. It's convenient to extend instantiation from regions to the things that occupy them. To say that this particular thing instantiates this eidolon means that the region occupied by that thing instantiates that eidolon. To say this oak tree instantiates oakness means that its tree-shaped-region instantiates oakness. This tree-shaped-region instantiates oakness, treeness, plantness, and life. Likewise, this oak tree instantiates those eidolons. If a thing instantiates an eidolon, then it *participates* in that eidolon; the eidolon is *present in* or *at* the thing.

[19] This metaphysics entails substantivalism about space, eternalism about time, and perdurantism about persistence.

[20] Space-time is not material stuff. Material stuff (matter) does not exist. This is not hylomorphism.

[21] Cellular automatons put machines at points or point-sized regions, and severely restrict their communicative relations. But eidolon systems put machines at all regions of space-time, and allow them to communicate in all possible ways. They are vastly more powerful than cellular automatons.

Following the Platonists, I say *instantiation takes degrees*. A line drawn with a ruler instantiates linearity more than a line drawn by hand. A diamond has hardness to a greater degree than a stick of butter. Every thing instantiates every eidolon to some degree between 0 and 1. Degrees can be vague (i.e. they need not be defined as exact numbers).[22] Eidolons are more or less present in the things that more or less instantiate them. Hence degrees of presence are *strong* or *weak*. Strong presence is degree 1; weak is any positive degree less than 1. Absence is degree 0; it is not a degree of presence. When I use the term *degree*, I mean some degree of presence, some positive degree. Thus an oak strongly instantiates oakness; Hypatia strongly instantiates womanhood, personhood, and so on. The degree to which an eidolon is present in some thing is its similarity to those things in which the eidolon is strongly present. The degree to which oakness is present in any thing is its similarity to any oak. If any eidolon is present in any thing in any (positive) degree, then it is wholly, entirely, or integrally present in that thing. Since foxes are similar to dogs, foxness is *entirely but weakly* present in every dog. The souls of things include only eidolons which are strongly present in those things. The soul of Socrates includes eidolons like life, animality, mammalness, humanity, maleness, and so on. The soul of Socrates contains all the biological eidolons encoded in his genome.

Since every thing in Nature exists, every thing strongly instantiates Isness. Hence Isness is *omnipresent*. And since Isness is wholly present in every thing, it is an *integrally omnipresent* power. But every eidolon is a specialization of Isness; hence every eidolon is also integrally omnipresent (Plotinus, *Enneads*, 6.4–5). Moreover, since every thing has some degree of similarity to every other thing, again every eidolon is present to some degree in every thing. Integral omnipresence means that every eidolon is wholly present in every thing to some positive degree. The maximal productivity of Isness entails that for any eidolon, and any region of any space-time in any universe, that region instantiates that eidolon to some positive degree. That positivity may be extremely small. These ideas recall Anaxagoras, who thought the “seeds” of all things are present in all things.

Of course, since things are different, different eidolons must be present in them to different degrees. The eidolon plantness is strongly present in every plant, but only weakly present in every animal, and barely present at all in rocks. Here the energy theory of animism confirms the vitality theory: every space-time region (every thing) instantiates life to some positive degree, and is

22 A finite-precision decimal is a vague number, which covers the real numbers that round up or down to it.

therefore alive to some positive degree. Although an *organism* is a space-time region that strongly instantiates life (its soul includes life), yet life is wholly present (even if only weakly present) in every thing. Since quarks are not strongly alive, their souls do not include life. Nevertheless, every quark is alive in some small degree. Life is wholly present in every atom, star, planet, rock, and so on. Since the same points apply for mentality and personhood, the energy theory confirms the mentality theory. Every thing instantiates mentality and personality to some degree. A *mind* is any region which strongly instantiates mentality; its soul includes mentality. A *person* is any region which strongly instantiates personhood; its soul includes personhood. Yet mentality and personhood are wholly (even if only weakly) present in every thing. Since rocks are not strongly persons, their souls do not include personhood. Yet personhood is weakly though wholly present in every rock. Personhood is entirely present in every rock, even though its full self-manifestation is frustrated by stronger eidolons.

Similar points apply to deities. Batty writes, "many a Witch will tell you that the spirit of every deity exists in every living thing. A tree may not look very feline, but the spirit of Bastet can be found in its living energy" (2023: 121–122). Bastet is the Egyptian goddess of cats. Her spirit is her soul, which is an eidolon. Since cats are sacred to Bastet, the soul of Bastet is strongly instantiated in every cat. Since trees resemble cats (they are both alive), the soul of Bastet is wholly weakly present in every tree. Likewise, Bastet is wholly weakly present in every thing. As Thales said, the world is full of gods.

Eidolons define *bodies* (aka *extensions*). The body of any eidolon is the whole composed of all things which *strongly* instantiate that eidolon. The body of plantness is the whole composed of all regions in which plantness is strongly present. Some wholes contain parts from many different universes (Lewis, 1986: ch. 4.3); these are transworld wholes. The *modally extended body* of an eidolon is the fusion (the union) of all of its bodies in all worlds. The modally extended body of plantness contains all plants in all possible universes. Possible universes inhabit logical space. If we think of logical space as an "astral" space, then modally extended bodies are *astral bodies*.

The eidolons in your body are entangled with all the eidolons in your environment. One way to become aware of these entanglements, which is deeply sensory, involves *mindful immersion* in the nonhuman environment (Starhawk, 1999: 8–9, 220, 274–275). Watson (2008) offers a sequence of powerful immersive Pagan nature meditations. Pagan generalists advocate careful sensory attention during nature walks (Beckett, 2017: 58, 137–138; Lupa, 2021: 28–35, 157–174; Wildermuth, 2021: 52, 188–190). Wiccans and witches likewise advocate spiritual exercises involving mindful attention to nature with all the senses (Crowley, 2001: 28–30, 50–51; Sylvan, 2012: 102; Murphy-Hiscock, 2017: 60–62, 69–74, ch. 4; Roderick, 2005 1, 12, 16, 181). These exercises might involve intensely focused sensory attention on instances of the four elements (Crowley, 2001: 28–30; Murphy-Hiscock, 2017: 65–69). Or close attention to the sun, moon, and stars (Beckett, 2017: 34, 141–142; Wildermuth, 2021: 15–24). Or close attention to seasonal changes (Crowley, 2001: 50–51). Druids also practice these immersive environmental rituals (Billington, 2011: ch. 2; Greer, 2021: 73–77, ch. 8). Nature-immersion can be more intense, including endurance running, surfing, and mountaineering.

3.4 Eidolons Strive to Produce their Instances

Powerful properties usually define *dispositions*. The charge carried by a particle disposes it to accelerate when placed in an electromagnetic field. Powerful properties (i.e. eidolons) are *oriented* or *directed towards* manifesting their dispositions, and all eidolons have this dispositional directedness. But if anything is directed, then there is something to which it is directed, namely, its *telos*. Here I use the term *teleomaticity* to refer to the dispositional directedness of eidolons. For physical eidolons, this directedness has been characterized as a kind of intentionality, often called *physical intentionality* (Bauer, 2016).[23] However, for consistency, I will say *teleomatic intentionality*.

Eidolons direct themselves towards manifesting their powers. But they most intensely manifest their powers through regions which strongly instantiate them. Therefore, if some eidolon is present in any region to any degree, then it drives that region to strongly instantiate that eidolon. Eidolons are *driving powers* or *driving forces*. Thus any region which contains any eidolon to any degree contains an internal force which drives it towards the finality (*telos*) of being a strong instance of that eidolon. Hence that region teleomatically *strives* to be a strong instance of the eidolon.[24] Since Isness flows outwards in a maximally powerful and positive way, the Isness in every eidolon directs it towards maximizing its self-manifestations through its strong self-instantiations. The Isness in every eidolon directs it to produce as many strong instances of itself as possible. This directedness, which emerges in the being of the eidolon, is its *teleomatic*

[23] Although I focus on physical forms, mathematical forms are also eidolons, and all these points apply to them as well. Mathematical eidolons are integrally omnipresent in Nature and therefore in our universe. They are causally powerful forms. The eidolon triangularity skillfully drives every thing to be a triangle; the number 5 skillfully drives every thing to have 5 as its cardinality. As Franklin says, "mathematical necessities constrain what is possible," and those constraints appear physically as inviolable forces (2015: 32–33). Pagans sensitive to mathematical forms practice *sacred geometry* and *sacred arithmetic* (Sabin, 2011: 28–29).

[24] Leibniz says possibilities strive (*On the Radical Origination of Nature*).

purpose. This is a kind of reproductive purposiveness, which makes eidolons more lifelike, but they are not alive. Things acquire the purposes of their eidolons. Since eidolons have purposes, they have positivities and negativities. It is *teleomatically good* for oakness to make more oaks; it is *teleomatically bad* for it to be frustrated in its oak-making project.

Since every eidolon is wholly present in every region, every region strives to be a strong instance of every eidolon. This rock strives to be a proton, a star, a bacterium, a tree, a human. But supersubstantivalism extends this striving to all space-time regions: every region strives to strongly instantiate every eidolon. This is a more profound animism: *space-time itself boils with eidetic strivings.* Since oakness is omnipresent on earth, it strives to realize its purpose by covering the earth with as many oaks as possible. It strives to turn everything into an oak. Since oakness is also omnipresent in the soil on Mars, that Martian soil also strives to self-organize into as many oaks as possible. But different eidolons are present to different degrees in any region. If the birdness in some region is stronger than the humanness in that region, then its striving to be a bird is greater than its striving to be a human. Stronger eidolons can defeat weaker eidolons. The birdness in this crow defeats the humanness in that crow. Since the oaky striving in the soil of Mars is defeated by many far more powerful eidolons, there are no oaks on Mars.

Supersubstantivalism helps to make sense of Pagan claims about the appearances of mythical organisms, such as elves, fairies, nymphs, and other "nature spirits." All these things are possible organisms. Although there are no actual elves on our earth, every region of space around us is teeming with elf-eidolons (elf-spirits) striving to produce elves in those regions. These strivings are strongest in elf-shaped regions. Over there, in the underbrush in the forest, there is an elf-shaped region which includes some leaves twirling near a rock. The motions in that region briefly permit the elf-spirit to manifest itself more strongly, so an elf-eidolon briefly flashes into stronger presence there.

If you're looking, that brief flash into stronger presence may cause your brain to produce a representation of an elf. You may seem to see an elf. Of course, no elf exists there. Hence you are not *perceiving* an elf (you are not *seeing* it); on the contrary, you are *hallucinating* an elf. But modal realism allows hallucinations to be *truthful* (to be *veridical*). According to modal realism, hallucinations *truthfully represent* things in non-actual universes (Lewis, 1983; Averill & Gottlieb, 2021). When you hallucinate an elf, your brain represents a non-actual elf, that is, an elf in some other possible universe. Pagans often say that things like elves and fairies exist in some "otherworld," and modal realism explains how this makes sense. Elves (and fairies) exist in non-actual universes. Far from being meaningless errors, hallucinations have religious significance:

they reveal that Nature is much greater than our universe; they point to the self-transcendence of Nature. They reveal that Nature is that than which no greater is possible.

3.5 How Eidolons Have Directed Skills

Since eidolons are powers, they interact through power relations, namely, relations of *cooperation* and *competition*. Cooperative relations include support, excitation, assistance, and so on. Since plants and animals provide various services to each other, the eidolon plantness and the eidolon animality cooperate in some ways. Competitive relations include resistance, interference, blocking, and so on. Since plantness strives to change all things into plants, while animality strives to change all things into animals, animality and plantness compete in some ways. Eidolons form constraint satisfaction networks, in which they are connected by cooperative (excitatory) and competitive (inhibitory) links. Oakness requires cooperation from eidolons like water, organic chemistry, protection from radiation, and so on. On Mars, those are far too weak to support oaks.

When eidolons interact, they interact like the players in a game, who cooperate and compete. Hence eidolons resemble algorithms for playing games. Moreover, the striving of any eidolon to produce its instances resembles the striving of a game-player for winning their game. Based on these resemblances, I will say eidolons (spirits) are game-playing algorithms. A chess-playing program is a system of strategies for winning games of chess. The eidolon plantness is a plant-manifestation program, which is a system of strategies for manifesting all the causal powers of plants (photosynthesizing, extending its roots, taking in water, making leaves and seeds, and so on). Any eidolon has strategies for making strong self-instances. Plantness includes a plant-making program, a system of strategies for winning games of plant-making. Plantness aims to make plants like chess-programs aim to checkmate the opposing king. Within any thing, plantness is playing a game with every other eidolon. When plantness wins, a plant appears; when it loses, no plant appears. Usually, it loses; it gets outplayed by other eidolons, like hydrogen.

Algorithms for playing games have *competence or skill.* Chess programs have some chess-playing skill. Thus eidolons have a kind of *knowledge* (Bauer, 2022: ch. 6). Plantness has all the skillful know-how required for making and being a plant. However, as Dennett argues (2009) is possible to have *competence without comprehension*. The skill in any eidolon is a specialized form of *techne*. It is *arete*, that is, performative excellence or virtue. It is *arete* for making a strong self-instance. An eidolon is an algorithmically shaped specialization of Isness, which skillfully directs itself to the finality of producing a strong instance of itself. Since eidolons are specializations of Isness, and Isness is a maximally positive power, the skills of eidolons are *ideal*. Humanity, the eidolon that animates all humans, is the ideal skill of being human. Driven by this eidolon, every human aims at fully manifesting this ideal skill. Pagan ethics therefore includes the ethics of skillful praxis, that is, *virtue ethics* (York, 2015). This ideality helps to explain why deities are often portrayed as *ideally skilled* in specific domains (Athena is an ideal weaver, Apollo an ideal doctor, Artemis an ideal hunter, and so on).

Every eidolon is a specialization of Isness, which is purely wild power; but wildness implies *sovereignty*; therefore, every eidolon has its own sovereignty. Beckett says everything has "inherent sovereignty" (2019: 20). An eidolon is Isness constrained by its position in a network of relations. Hence the sovereignty of any eidolon is constrained by that of others; it is *bounded sovereignty*. Assuming that anything with sovereign power is an agent, eidolons are *teleomatic agents*. As such, they confer agency on their instances, which are likewise agents (Ellis, 2014: 3). Assuming further that sovereignty entails *duties* and *rights*, every eidolon has the duty and the right to try to change each thing into a strong instance of itself. Oakness has the duty and the right to try to change every thing into an oak. When eidolons compete, their rights come into conflict, and those conflicts must be resolved by justice. But the justice of wild sovereigns is wild justice.

As physical systems gain complexity, some of them gain life. Their souls include the life eidolon; they include the skills required for living in a specific way. Organisms encode their souls in their genetic programs; hence they give themselves their own laws, so they are self-governing and *autonomous*. To use an Aristotelian term, their genetic programs encode their *entelechies*. In organisms, teleomaticity evolves into *teleonomy*. Organisms have teleonomic intentionalities, purposes, power relations, skills, sovereignties, agencies, duties, rights, and so on. The teleonomic intentionality of an organism is its *will*. When its will sharpens itself into its most authentic form, it becomes *true will*. Teleonomy supports rich forms of functionality and normativity, providing a basis for ethics. Since all things instantiate life to some degree, all things participate in teleonomy.

Among living systems, mental properties and powers emerge, such as intelligence and consciousness. Perhaps all living systems have minds; perhaps only some do. Perhaps mentality extends beyond life, to robots or artificial intelligence. A mind is any space-time region which strongly instantiates the eidolon mentality (including eidolons like perception, intelligence, memory, and so on). In minds, teleonomy evolves into *teleology*, intelligent purposiveness. Some minds are persons. On one traditional analysis, the eidolon personhood includes rationality, moral responsibility, and teleological agency. Humans are persons, but there may be many other kinds. Yet all things wholly instantiate personhood to some degree. To some degree, ecosystems, rivers, mountains, the earth, the sun, and all things, are persons with all the qualities of personhood.

3.6 Freedom and Fate

The metaphysics of eidolons entails that humans (and other agents) have *constrained freedom*. On the one hand, since our eidolons have sovereignty, we have free will. On the other hand, since all eidolons have bounded sovereignty, our free will is constrained or limited. This thesis of limited free will is supported by many Paganisms. Wiccans affirm that we have free will (Crowley, 2001: 172, 2003: 70; Cunningham, 2004: 6, 74; Sylvan, 2012: 27–28, 45; Roderick, 2021: 150). Witches also affirm it (e.g. Batty, 2023: 118, 221). And free will is central to Asatru (Lafayllve, 2013: chs. 7 & 8; Nordvig, 2020: 53; Paxson, 2021: 136–138). On my readings, these Pagans are endorsing *libertarian freedom*: you have real choices; whatever you do, it is (almost) always the case that you could have done otherwise. Yet these Pagans also say that our freedom is constrained (see Lafayllve, 2013: chs. 7 & 8). Some aspects of our lives are fated, and our choices are constrained by our fates. For the Asatru, your fate is your *orlog*. But within the confines of your fate, you are free, and this freedom is your *wyrd*. Thus a river is free to move within the boundaries of its floodplain: "Orlog is the floodplain, and wyrd is the movement of the river" (Lafayllve, 2013: 103; Batty, 2023: 22–23). Sometimes your fate fully constrains your action, so that you have only one choice; but, almost always, you have many options.

The metaphysical picture that seems to provide the best support for the Pagan notion of constrained freedom is that of *branching space-time* (Belnap, 1992; Wronski & Placek, 2009; Muller, 2012). Here I do not defend or endorse branching space-time; I merely use it to analyze Pagan freedom. Branching space-time says that our universe is a cosmic tree of nodes linked by branches. Each node is the total 3D space of our universe at an instant of time. Every spatial region in every node instantiates every eidolon to some greater or lesser degree of strength. The initial node (the root of the tree) is the big bang. Every node sprouts branches which lead to other nodes. Every linear path through the tree is a 4D history of our universe, and these histories overlap.[25] These histories are not distinct universes or worlds but are the many variant histories within a single universe.

[25] A non-deterministic universe (like ours) has many overlapping but distinct histories. But a purely deterministic universe (like some game of life) has exactly one history.

These branching histories support local modalities of necessity and contingency, and these modalities support constrained freedom (Belnap, 2005). Fate is local necessity: if you are fated to do an act, then it occurs on all your future histories. Freedom is local contingency. If you are free to get married or stay single, then on some future histories you are married, and on others you are not. Of course, your fate can be specific: you are fated to marry this particular person. Or it can be vague: on all your future branches, you get married, but to different people on different branches. Thus branching space-time provides a good model for Lafayllve's discussion of time (2013: ch. 8). She says, "every decision made in the present will impact which of several potential futures will occur" (2013: 111). These potential futures lie within distinct histories in our cosmic tree. And the Pagan notion of the world tree (Yggdrasil) supports the notion of branching space-time.

Branching space-time models often distinguish between realized and unrealized histories. At least one history is realized, while the others are merely unrealized potentials. For Pagans, wyrd flows like a river down each realized history. Thus wyrd is some specialized power of Isness, which confers realization. On my readings of the branching space-time literature, realization is some greater intensity of existence. Organisms in realized histories have self-locating awareness (Placek, 2012). A realized version of your body has the indexical awareness that *I am here now*. All organisms participate in time as an objective B-series (earlier, simultaneous, later) of events, but realized organisms also indexically participate in it as a subjectively flowing A-series (past, present, future) of events (Farr, 2012). Perhaps these points entail that things in unrealized histories lack consciousness, while things in realized histories have it. Perhaps there are other ways to cash out the difference between realized and unrealized histories. Fortunately, we don't need a fully worked out theory of this difference here.

The branching space-time model says you have many possible life histories, and the free will to selectively realize some lives while leaving others unrealized. Your possible lives are more or less closely aligned with your *true will*. Beckett says your true will is your essence; it is your destiny and your calling (2017: 211). And "True will is your reason for being in this world, what you need to accomplish while you're here" (2017: 190). Sabin says your true will is "the force that drives you to your ultimate spiritual goal"; it drives you to "act according to your highest purpose" (2011: 36). She says that, when your will aligns with your true will, you are fully self-realized, and you are maximally harmonized with mundane things and with the deities (2011: 38). Lives (and actions) more closely aligned with your true will are more authentic and virtuous. They more intensely express the unique excellence of your soul (Crowley, 2003: ch. 13).

4 Theologies

4.1 The Archaic Theology

The oldest Pagan theology, call it the *archaic theology*, says the deities (gods and goddesses) are superhuman animals. Archaic Greeks pictured the Olympians as superhuman animals, that is, as living physical bodies that are similar but functionally superior to humans (Osborne, 2010; Hedreen, 2021). Epicurus argued that the deities are superhuman animals (Cicero, *On the Nature of the Gods*, I.46–9, I.67–9). Plotinus affirmed physical deities who walk the earth (*Enneads*, 2.9.8.30–35, 5.1.4.4–5, 5.3.17.30–32, 5.8.2.12–15, 6.5.12.30–35, etc.). The Norse deities were portrayed as superhuman animals (Taggart, 2019).[26] According to the archaic theology, the deities have sexual bodies, and they love having sex. They have parents and children. They eat and drink. They love partying and violent combat. Athena smashes Ares' skull with a rock (*Illiad*, 21.392–426). The hand of the Norse god Tyr is bitten off by the wolf Fenrir.

To say the deities are superhuman animals means at least three things. First, it means that, *for any positive property of human animality, the deities have that property in some greater degree.* On any measure of physiological excellence, their bodies are superior to all human bodies. For any animal skill, they are more skillful than us. They are faster, stronger, healthier, longer-lived, sexier, smarter, more virtuous, and so on. However, the deities are finite, not maximally perfect (e.g. Lafayllve, 2013: 24–27; Beckett, 2017: ch. 4; Greer, 2023: 51). They are not omnipotent, omniscient, omnibenevolent, or omni- anything else. Second, it means that, *for any negative property of human animality, they have that property in some lesser degree.* They are less vulnerable to injury, illness, aging, and death. Yet less vulnerable does not mean invulnerable. The Olympians get injured (and cured). The Norse deities get injured, and they will die. Third, superhumanity means that the deities resemble us: they are super-*human* (York, 2003: 13). They are *Homo deus*, that is, another species in the biological genus *Homo* (Harari, 2015: 53).

The archaic theology entails that the deities are natural physical things. They are neither disembodied minds nor immaterial persons. Many contemporary Pagans repeat the archaic theme that deities belong to our natural physical universe (Starhawk, 1999: 22; Beckett, 2017: 195; Sebastiani, 2020: 64; Wildermuth, 2021: 152; Greer, 2023: 86, see 13).[27] Contemporary Pagans

---

26 Heidegger suggests a Germanic polytheism, in which the deities are aesthetic-pragmatic features of being-in-the-world (Vanhala, 2014; Travers, 2018). Plebuch (2010) links Heideggerian polytheism to Asatru.

27 *Fictionalism* has been used to analyze Pagan polytheism (Palmqvist, 2023). *Simulationism* (the thesis that we are living in a computer simulation) can support a polytheistic theology (Bostrom, 2003; Chalmers, 2022). Since I am not aware of any Pagans who adopt these theologies, I do not

almost universally declare that Paganisms are nature religions, so that Pagans are committed to science. Beckett says, "A commitment to nature is a commitment to science" (2017: 40). So here I assume that Pagan deities have scientifically definable physical bodies of some kind. They may inhabit other possible universes, and their bodies may be very strange. Perhaps they are bodies of pure quantum information or pure holographic light. Yet they remain physical bodies. Nevertheless, there does not seem to be any evidence for the past or present existence of any divine bodies on our earth or even in our universe as far as we understand it.

4.2 The Modal Realist Theology

According to the *modal realist theology*, the divine bodies live in other possible universes. Although Pagans do not explicitly discuss modal realism, they often do refer to an otherworld or to many other worlds. Since Nature is a maximally great network (Section 2.4), it contains many possible universes. David Lewis, the main architect of modal realism, has developed this modal realist theology (Steinhart, 2023). Although Lewis denies that our universe contains any deities, he affirms that other universes do contain deities. Thor exists in another possible universe (Lewis, 2020: Ltr. 205). In their own universes, the deities are natural superhuman animals. Hence this theology agrees with the archaic theology that the deities are divine bodies.

Modal realism provides an argument for the existence of Pagan deities: (1) Although the Norse deities (the Aesir and Vanir) do not actually exist, it is possible that they exist. (2) But if it is possible that some things exist, then there are possible universes in which they do exist. (3) Therefore, there are non-actual possible universes in which the Aesir and Vanir exist. Since the Norse deities do not actually exist, when the stories about them are recited here, they are recited as *fiction* (they are the Norse *myths*). However, since there are universes where those deities do exist, and where they do what the stories portray them as doing, there are universes where the Norse myths are told as known fact. The myths are *veridical fictions* (Lewis, 1978). The existence of universes with Pagan deities is consistent with science, so the Lewisian polytheism is naturalistic in that sense.

The Pagan thesis of universal interconnection entails that the possible universes are all highly interrelated. And while they are not spatially, temporally, or causally interrelated, modal realism says that things in one universe have *counterparts* in other universes. Counterparts share the same essence, but they vary in their details. There are many possible versions of Odin, who differ in

include them here. But both fictionalism and simulationism affirm that the deities are superhuman animals.

their nonessential details. One version of Odin sacrificed his eye at the well of Mimir, while another version did not. These are two different Odins, namely, Odin-1 and Odin-2. These two Odins are counterparts of each other. Since modal realism says that possible worlds do not overlap (they share no parts), these two Odins live in two distinct worlds, namely, Asgard-1 and Asgard-2. But each Odin lives in exactly one possible world. Counterparts are maximally similar; hence they share the same maximally specific eidolon, the same maximally specific essence. Since the maximally specific eidolon of any organism is its soul, the counterparts of organisms share the same soul (or its upgraded versions). Hence we have counterparts in other universes. Your counterpart in some other universe shares your soul (your form, not your mind).

You have counterparts in universes inhabited by deities. Since it is possible for you to feast with Odin in Asgard, you have a counterpart who does feast with Odin there. Through our counterparts, we *vicariously act* in other universes. Through your counterpart in Asgard, you *vicariously feast* with Odin, although you may not be aware of it. We become aware of our vicarious interactions with the deities by ritually simulating our counterparts who interact with them. Such simulations involve *live-action role-playing* (*larping*), and Neopagan rituals are said to resemble larping (Ramstedt, 2007). Just as we have counterparts in divine universes, so the deities have counterparts in our universe. And, if we vicariously interact with otherworldly deities via our counterparts in their universes, then *the deities vicariously interact with us* via their counterparts in our actual universe.

Although humans have related to their deities in many ways, one of these ways is especially suited to the modal realist theology: *the deities are ideals*.[28] We ought to aspire and strive to become more like them. We act religiously when we orient ourselves towards the deities by imitating them. The religious practice known as *theurgy* aimed to make humans more divine. Theurgy is consistent with the archaic and modal realist theologies. If deities are in other universes, they can function perfectly well as regulative ideals. This theurgical religion is nicely illustrated by an old Wiccan maxim: when anyone bows down to the Goddess, the Goddess says, "Rise!" (see Sylvan, 2012: 31). Even when dealing with the deities, we are persons with inherent worth, dignity, autonomy, and sovereignty (Beckett, 2017: 76, 83–84). Of course, the theurgical view that the deities are ideals includes praising, honoring, and revering them. We ought to be religiously devoted to our ideals, so that a theurgical Paganism opens up a wide range of useful religious behaviors.

[28] Nietzsche and William James suggest that deities are personifications of ideal value-patterns (Dreyfus & Kelly, 2011; Larvor, 2020; Rodgers, 2020).

4.3 The Big Powers Theology

The *big powers theology* says the deities are large-scale natural causal powers or their domains (their extensions). On this theology, *the deities are eidolons of immense power.* Cicero says Demeter is the universal power (Isness) specialized into plantness (an eidolon); Apollo is the universal power specialized into stars (*On the Nature of the Gods,* II.71). More recently, Greer writes that for the ancient Greeks “the atmosphere was in some sense the body of Zeus; Demeter’s body was the soil, Poseidon’s the ocean” (2019: 24). He proposes that “a god of weather could be conceptualized as the indwelling consciousness of the lower atmosphere itself” (2023: 91). O’Donoghue says, “a god might be the mind that arises from a forest, a river, a planet or a cluster of galaxies” (2022: 25). Byghan says that for Druids the deities are “a living, vibrant entity or group of entities that is or are immanent in all things, from quarks to constellations” (2018: 6).

According to the big powers theology, the deities are divine souls. Since the deities are alive, their souls contain the eidolons of life to superhuman degrees. Since the deities are persons, their souls contain the eidolons of personhood to superhuman degrees. Of course, eidolons themselves, as causally powerful universals, are neither alive nor personal. It is the *instances* of those eidolons that are alive and personal. Demeter is a superhuman soul. Demeter is an eidolon which is instantiated to some degree by every space-time region in every universe. Many regions merely weakly instantiate Demeter. Nevertheless, since that divine soul is so powerful, even the weak presence of Demeter in some region may be more powerful than the strong presence of lesser eidolons. If the Demeter-soul is weakly present in any region, it strives to turn it into an instance of the body of Demeter, into a plant. It strives to turn it into a region in which she is strongly present. The deities are hardly far away. Everything around you is a *weak avatar* of every deity.

Ancient Pagans portray the deities as active in particular domains. The domain of Zeus is the sky with its storms; Poseidon gets the oceans; Demeter gets the plants; Artemis gets the animals. Likewise, in Norse Paganism, the domain of Sif is the plants; Eir gets health; Freyr gets male sexuality and fertility; Tyr gets war and justice. Each deity is strongly instantiated in every region in its domain. Our earthly *botanosphere* is the totality of earthly plants. It is a space-time region with a very complicated shape. Sif and Demeter are both strongly present in every subregion in our botanosphere. Poseidon is strongly present in every subregion of the ocean; Tyr and Athena are strongly present in every region which contains conflicts and their resolutions. Any region in which a deity is strongly present is a *body* of that deity. It is a *theophany* of the deity. A theophany is a *strong avatar* of a deity; it is a strong avatar of some divine soul. Of course, since eidolons are wholly present in their instances, every deity is wholly present in its theophany. Sif is wholly present in this leaf, in this tree, in this jungle, in the whole botanosphere.

The deities are eidolons, but eidolons are causal powers; causal powers fully manifest themselves wherever they are strongly present; hence the deities are active in their theophanies. Zeus is active in every region of the atmosphere; Sif is active in every part of the botanosphere. Thus Sif sprouts, sends down roots, sends up branches and leaves, photosynthesizes, flowers, and makes seeds. If that is right, then the body of Sif takes on many different spatio-temporal shapes. This is consistent with the lore, which portrays many deities as shape-shifters. Yet Sif, like every deity, is an extraordinarily powerful mind. But how does that cohere with the thesis that Sif photosynthesizes? The answer is that causal powers are algorithmic. The mind of Sif runs every earthly botanical computation. These computations define the dynamical physical activities in every leaf, plant, forest, and jungle. Zeus runs a computation which generates the entire atmospheric process for our earth. Poseidon computes the entire process of the oceans.

Sallustius associates the deities with very deep natural powers (*On the Gods and the World*, ch. 6). Hence the bodies of deities can be very deep natural processes.[29] Some very potent divine bodies are found in mathematical physics. Wen (2018) proposes that our universe supervenes on an ocean of entangled bits of quantum information. If such an ocean exists, it is a deep body of Poseidon. Likewise thermodynamic irreversibility is a deep body of Hades. Irreversibility brings death, but without it, life would not exist at all. The myths poetically portray Hekate as dwelling in an underworld beneath the earth. More deeply, the Underworld inside every black hole is a body of Hekate. Since every black hole contains a body of Hekate, her eternally unblinking eye stares out from all our black holes, watching our cosmic tapestry unfold. Hekate collapses the wave function (Danielson et al., 2022). She algorithmically exercises her causal power by collapsing the wave function, and without her action, the wave function would not collapse. As Plato said, our universe is a "shrine for the ever-living gods" (*Timaeus*, 37 c).

Since deities are eidolons, and eidolons have instances in all possible universes, the deities have instances in all possible universes. A *transworld whole*

[29] The Wiccan God has theophanies (the sun, wild animals, hunting, etc.), while the Goddess has theophanies (the earth or moon, the maiden-mother-crone, plants, etc.). However, the Wiccan God and Goddess are often defined as immanent powers in nature, as aspects of the power of the Wiccan One (Farrar & Farrar, 1981: 49; Buckland, 1986: 19–21; Cantrell, 2001: 24–28; Crowley, 2003: 227–228; Cunningham, 2004: 9, 14; Cuhulain, 2011: 14; Sabin, 2011: 26, 117; Silver Elder, 2011: 9, 18). Hence it may be more accurate to say they are powers rather than deities.

has parts taken from many universes. So the transworld whole composed of all the possible bodies of any deity is its *transworld body*. This is its modally extended body. But Paganism has another term: possible universes are located in logical space; if logical space is *astral space*, then the transworld whole composed of all the avatars of any deity is its *astral body*. The astral body of Sif includes all possible botanospheres; the astral body of Hekate includes all the black holes in all possible universes; the astral body of Apollo includes all stars in all universes. Since the lore portrays the deities as superhuman primates, there are universes in which they are strongly instantiated in superhuman bodies. There are universes in which Demeter is strongly present in some body of the species *Homo olympianus*, and universes in which Sif is strongly present in some body of the species *Homo aesirus*. Of course, if Sif and Demeter are different deities, then their bodies differ in some possible way. All these considerations show that the big powers theology includes both the archaic theology and the modal realist theology. So I adopt the big powers theology here.

Humans adopt many religious behaviors towards the deities. These include praise, thanksgiving, meditations, prayers, worship, sacrificial offerings, and so on. Acts of praise and thanksgiving are appropriately directed towards eidolons. It is proper to praise Apollo for the life-giving radiance of the sun and to thank Sif for the bounty of the harvest. It is appropriate to meditate on the Zeus-power in the sky, and to engage Athena or Tyr in contemplative prayer and philosophical reflection. The eidolon theology makes sense of petitionary prayers. Thor is weakly present in my brain. Even though Thor is weak in my brain, Thor is a god, and the Thor-eidolon is extremely powerful. The Thor-eidolon has extremely great powers of perception (powers to gather information), and, through his instantiation in my brain, Thor perceives all my mental activities. If I pray to Thor, he hears me. If the intention of my petition coheres with his intentions and serves the greater harmonies of the deities, then he may incorporate the intentionality of my petition into his own intentionality, so the goal of my prayer becomes more probable. By performing acts of worship and sacrifice, we show our social commitments to the deities. We indicate our intention to align our own communal actions with the divine harmonies. As our intentions become more aligned with those of the deities, they are more likely to bear fruit. Of course, we can also show our devotion to the deities by caring for the things in their domains. You can show your devotion to Sif by caring for plant life. You can show your reverence to Zeus by working for justice, by working to mitigate air pollution and climate change. You can venerate Thor by caring for our whole earthly ecosystem.

4.4 Religious Experiences

Pagans have religious experiences. Beckett describes a religious experience in which he seemed to see "a green glowing bird" (2019: 17). While this bird appeared to be located here on earth, he did not describe it as an *actual* bird. He described it as "the Otherworld is bleeding over into the ordinary world" (Beckett, 2016). A bird from another world appeared in ours. Since no actual bird was involved, his experience was not a perception, but a hallucination. However, hallucinations can be *truthful*, that is, veridical.

One way to analyze the truthfulness of religious experiences starts with eidolons. Beckett was looking at some region of space-time in our universe. At that region, the *green-glowing-bird* eidolon was striving to produce a strong instance of itself. And, lacking sufficient supportive relations with the other eidolons there, its strivings mostly failed. However, for a brief instant, those relations became more supportive, so the green-glowing-bird eidolon flashed into greater strength. Beckett saw that region, in an abrupt and irregular way, more strongly instantiating the green-glowing-bird eidolon. It was an *epiphany*: a flashing into greater than usual presence. Still, that eidolon did not become strongly instantiated, so Beckett was not looking at any particular green glowing bird. That region only weakly instantiated the green-glowing-bird eidolon. That flash of the bird eidolon into greater strength caused Beckett to hallucinate.

According to modal realism, hallucination involves several components (Lewis, 1983; Averill & Gottlieb, 2021).[30] First, when a human has a hallucination of some thing, then that thing exists in some other possible universe. So the green glowing bird exists in some nonactual universe (call it Bird World). The region in our universe at which the glowing green bird eidolon flashed into greater strength is a counterpart of that bird in Bird World. Through its counterpart in our universe, the glowing green bird in Bird World *vicariously perched and flew* here on earth. Second, the hallucinating human has a counterpart in that other universe who is *perceiving* that thing. So Beckett has a counterpart (call him Bird Beckett) in the Bird World, and Bird Beckett is perceiving (seeing) the green glowing bird. Third, a hallucinating human is *simulating* their otherworldly counterpart. So Actual Beckett simulates Bird Beckett. He is *vicariously seeing* through the eyes of his counterpart in another universe. These three components entail that, when Actual Beckett hallucinated his bird, he was truthfully representing a bird in another universe by simulating his perceiving counterpart in that other universe.

[30] The modal realist account raises several questions: Are all hallucinations veridical? If not, are there ways to distinguish between veridical and non-veridical hallucinations? And can we hallucinate impossible objects? These are deep questions, but I do not have space to go into these questions.

But why think these hallucinations are religious? An answer comes from the theory of astral bodies. Actual Beckett and Bird Beckett are avatars of each other. They are both parts of a larger astral body, which contains all their avatars in all possible universes. When you have a hallucination, you experience, in a forceful way, that you have an astral body, a body infinitely larger than your actual body. Since your astral body is not restricted to any particular universe (it is not "worldbound"), it *transcends* every universe. While bodies in universes are in space-times, astral bodies are *eternal*. Your body was born and it will die, but your astral body was never born and it will never die. Your astral body is *sublime*, and *numinous*, and therefore *awe-inspiring*. When you simulate a counterpart in some other universe, you virtually step outside of your own body, and that stepping outside of your body is *ek-stasis*, it is *ecstatic*. If an ecstatic experience reveals your participation in something with all these qualities, then it seems fair to call it religious. Of course, religious visions include visions of divine bodies, and such visions are also epiphanies. If you have a religious vision of the divine body of Athena in some space-time region, then her soul briefly flashes into greater strength at that region. The presence of her soul there becomes strong enough that it causes your brain to hallucinate her divine body. Your brain truthfully depicts the body of Athena in another universe.

4.5 Reincarnation and Deification

Ancient Platonists argued that humans can be reincarnated into deities. Most Paganisms affirm some kind of reincarnation (Starhawk, 1999: 51; Beckett, 2017: 33; Sebastiani, 2020: 91–92; Greer, 2023: ch. 9). Modern Hellenists affirm it (Alexander, 2007: 29–30). Druids affirm it (Byghan, 2018: 18–22). Wiccans clearly affirm reincarnation (Farrar & Farrar, 1981: 113; Buckland, 1986: 25–28; Starhawk, 1999: 110, 124–125; Cunningham, 2004: 73; Roderick, 2005: 54–55; Sabin, 2011: 31; Batty, 2023: Lesson 15). Witches affirm it too (Alexander, 2014: 19; Squire, 2021: 23). Some versions of Asatru affirm reincarnation (Paxson, 2021: 138–140).

Reincarnation usually involves souls. Any Paganism which centers itself in nature will aim for a naturalistic theory of the soul. Aristotle provided such a theory when he defined the soul as the form of the body (*De Anima,* 412a5-414a33). The Pagan metaphysics developed here affirms this Aristotelian theory: forms are eidolons, and your soul is the most specific eidolon which animates your body (Section 3.2). Your soul is mostly encoded in your DNA and in the neural network in your brain. Your soul is analogous to a software program, which can run on many different hardware computers.

Since your soul is a pattern, it can be transferred to some other physical medium. The pattern in your DNA can be copied into a clone. Buckland (1986: 26) suggests that earthly souls are reincarnated in bodies on other planets. Reincarnation may occur across universes (Steinhart, 2014, 2022: ch. 9). If your soul will be reincarnated into other bodies in other universes, which in turn will be reincarnated again, then all those iterated reincarnations are your counterparts, and they are parts of your astral body. Reincarnation asserts that, for every soul, if that soul is instantiated in some body in some universe, then some modified new soul will be instantiated in a modified new body in some modified new universe. The modification follows the laws of karma.

Pagans often affirm reciprocity, and the laws of karma are laws of reciprocity across lives. On the one hand, *retributive karmic laws* follow the maxim of "an eye for an eye, a tooth for a tooth." Since retributive karmic laws lead to endless cycles of evil returned for evil, any Paganism committed to justice must reject them. On the other hand, *progressive karmic laws* aim at moral rehabilitation and improvement. Kardec (1857) developed a theory of progressive karma; his theory inspired some Wiccans (Buckland, 1986: 26–27). Steinhart provides a detailed analysis of progressive karma (2022: ch. 9.6). Your soul will be upgraded, its vices evolved into virtues, its functions gaining greater powers. Your upgraded souls will run on upgraded bodies, eventually becoming deities.

5 The Arts of Possibility

5.1 Divination

All Pagan traditions include *divination*, performed by a *diviner*, who uses various techniques to allegedly gain information about the future. Divination includes activities like interpreting the positions of celestial bodies (astrology) or interpreting the motions of birds. It may use other natural objects, such as stones, feathers, bones, sticks, or herbs. Divination includes activities like reading tarot cards, or runes, or the I Ching. It may use other artifacts, like pendulums, mirrors, or bowls of water.

Divination is often thought of as fortune-telling, which aims to reliably provide accurate descriptions of the future. Some Pagans portray divination as fortune-telling (e.g. Buckland, 1986: 157; Alexander, 2014: 125; Greer, 2021: ch. 10; Batty, 2023: 216–217). In parallel with the distinction between high and low magic (see Sections 5.2–5.3), fortune-telling is *low divination*. While there are scientific objections to low divination, Pagans often raise another objection. Low divination relies heavily on the assumption that the future of our universe is clearly determined by its past. But the Pagan metaphysics of Section 3.6 says our universe has a branching space-time structure. From any present moment, it almost always happens that many future histories unfold. Our universe is highly nondeterministic, and, while fate usually *constrains*, it rarely *determines*. Pagans object that the future is far too open for low divination to have much success (Buckland, 1986: 157; Billington, 2011: 241; Lafayllve, 2013: ch. 8; Beckett, 2019: 63). Of course, some events are fated. You will die; the sun will rise tomorrow; entropy will increase.

By contrast, high divination has little interest in forecasting the future (that's a job for science). High divination is neither prophecy nor fortune-telling (Starhawk, 1999: 183–184; Billington, 2011: 241; Beckett, 2019: 63; Sebastiani, 2020: 104, 127–128). On the contrary, it helps you with self-realization. High divination helps you to clarify your intentionality and to ensure that your actions are authentic (Starhawk, 1999: 240, 274; Billington, 2011: 241; Sylvan, 2012: 133; Roderick, 2021: 296–327). For example, while *horoscopes* (as low divination) aim to forecast your day, *spiritual astrology* (as high divination) uses celestial patterns as question-raising tools to find your authentic agency. High divination helps you to see which of your possible futures most closely aligns with your true will (Sabin, 2011: 202; Beckett, 2017: 201). During high divination, you ultimately ask this question: *Which possible course of action aligns best with my true will?*

Of course, even though high divination is not fortune-telling, it still requires some information about the future. One way to gain such information (the scientific way) extends past regularities into the future. It traces the patterns in *forwards causal chains*, which run from past to future. But divination (low or high) does not use such chains. As a rule (I know of no exceptions), *divinatory practices begin with randomization*. Tarot cards are randomly shuffled; bones or runes are randomly thrown; coins and yarrow stalks randomly cast to read the I Ching; pendulums wobble. Astrology randomly assigns meanings to natal charts and celestial configurations. Since randomization scrambles regularities carried by forwards chains, starting divinatory processes with randomness entails that *forwards causal regularities do not persist into the divinatory process* (Scriven, 1956). Hence divinatory processes are not influenced by the past or present. It seems likely that the Pagan thesis of universal interconnection entails that all physical events are causally produced. If that is right, then the causal chains that produce divinatory outputs (like a tarot spread or an I Ching hexagram) come from the future. They are *backwards* or *retro-causal chains*. Hence divinatory outputs cards carry signals from the future. Divinatory practices are techniques for receiving signals from the future.

Many philosophers argue for backwards causal chains (Dummett, 1964). Backwards causality is often portrayed as one of the strange implications of quantum physics (Dowe, 1997; Evans, 2015). Of course, some philosophers and physicists reject backwards causation (Ben-Yami, 2007). Here I do not claim that backwards causality really exists; I merely use the theory of backwards causation to try to understand divination. Since backwards causality is natural, *divination is based on entirely natural physical processes*; it does not involve any bodiless minds, nor any supernatural intelligences, nor anything paranormal or psychic.[31] Just as forwards causal chains naturally carry meaningful signals along histories from the past into the future, so also backwards causal chains naturally carry meaningful signals along histories from the future into the past.

The Pagan thesis of universal interconnection provides an argument for backwards causation. It entails that all regions in all histories in our branching space-time are connected to each other. Hence regions in all our future histories are connected to regions in our pasts. On the analysis of animism presented in Section 3, all these regions instantiate eidolons. Eidolons in one region exert their causal powers on eidolons in other regions. If the causal powers of eidolons located at future regions fail to exert their powers on eidolons located at past regions, then eidetic causality is incomplete. But if that causality is incomplete, then the power of the One fails to maximize. Since that power does maximize, the network of causes in our universe contains causal chains that run both from the past into the future as well as causal chains that run from the future into the past.

Again, high divination aims to answer this question: Which possible course of action aligns best with my true will? When you ask that question, you are most receptive to (most *attuned* to) signals from the future which answer it, that is, to signals positively correlated with your true will. Those signals are eidolons from the future which become instantiated in the divinatory output (the tarot spread, the hexagram, etc.). Your attunement entails that those eidolons which become most strongly instantiated in the output are those which are most closely aligned with your true will. Through those eidolons, high divination most strongly reveals that course of action which aligns best with your true will. Assuming that you ought to act in accordance with your true will (Section 6.2), divination shows you what you ought to do. It reveals your most authentic course of action.

But the future is complex, so the outputs from high divination are not simplistic. High divination typically produce outputs which are semantically dense; it makes riddles and enigmas; it makes works of art with highly

[31] Some Wiccans do say divination uses psychic powers (Crowley, 2001: 58; Cunningham, 2004: 209; Roderick, 2005: 296; Batty, 2023: 216–217). It is a kind of precognition. And philosophers have argued that precognition can be explained naturalistically by backward causation (e.g. Mackie, 1966; Marwaha & May, 2016).

encrypted meanings. High divinatory works of art provide you with sensory and conceptual contents which help you to gain insights into your true will. For example, tarot cards are complex pictures; tarot guide books associate those pictures with dense networks of concepts. Using high divination to gain insight into your true will requires using aesthetic skills and sensitivities to interpret the divinatory outputs. These are sensitivities and skills for self-analysis. Taking an idea from the aesthetics of Noe (2018), divinatory practices are *strange tools*. They are tools for asking deep questions about the alignment of your will with your true will.

5.2 Defining Magic

Another way Pagans deal with the future is through *magic*. Although magic appears in almost every form of Paganism, different traditions place more or less emphasis on it. It is not thematized much in Druidry. Although magic was central to ancient Greco-Roman religion, Hellenists and Neoplatonic revivalists don't talk about it much. It plays a small role in Asatru (Lafayllve, 2013: ch. 10; Nordvig, 2020: ch. 6; Paxson, 2021: ch. 9). Yet magic is central to Wicca and witchcraft, so I will focus on its uses there.

While there are many Pagan definitions of magic, the classical definition comes from Aleister Crowley.[32] He says, "Magick is the Science and Art of causing Change to occur in conformity with Will" (1929: *xvi*). Many Pagans adopt Crowley's definition directly (e.g. Sabin, 2011: 30; Beckett, 2017: 190; Wildermuth, 2021: 157; Batty, 2023: 201). Many others start with it and modify it to make their own. I will use Crowley's definition here. Although some Pagans who use his definition may pick up a few elements from Crowley's elaborate metaphysics, most regard the definition as standing alone.

As the "Science and Art of causing Change to occur in conformity with Will," magic explicitly includes science. It therefore includes the scientifically well-validated practical techniques we use to achieve our goals. If you drink a glass of water to satisfy your thirst, then you are "causing Change to occur in conformity with Will", and that is magical. To refer to scientifically validated techniques, many Pagans use the term *mundane* (Roderick, 2005; Sabin, 2011; Sylvan, 2012; Beckett, 2017; Murphy-Hiscock, 2017; Batty, 2023; etc.). Although magic includes mundane practices, it usually refers to nonmundane practices like spellcasting and visualization. These techniques belong to the "Art" side of Crowley's definition. I will also use "magic" to refer to these arts.

Pagans often distinguish between two kinds of magic (Starhawk, 1999: 137–139; Crowley, 2001: 56; Sabin, 2011: 18, 31, 196; Beckett, 2017: 196–198). The

[32] Crowley 2001 and 2003 are by Vivianne Crowley, no relation to Aleister.

lower or lesser magic is instrumental. It resembles mundane technology but uses means (laws and forces) currently unknown to science (Starhawk, 1999: 37, 93; Cantrell, 2001: 160–164; Crowley, 2001: ch. 4; Cunningham, 2004: 22–23; Sebastiani, 2020: 95–102). To say the lower magic *works* means that it produces its intended outcome: a spell cast to get money to pay a bill works if and only if you get the money to pay the bill (Cunningham, 2004: 23–24).

Lower magic works by entirely natural means (Starhawk, 1999: 93; Cunningham, 2004: 6; Alexander, 2014: 19; Beckett, 2017: 195–197; Murphy-Hiscock, 2017: 14; Roderick, 2021: 3–6; Wildermuth, 2021: 152).[33] Magic does not involve commanding supernatural persons. Lower magic utilizes the entanglements among natural powers (Plotinus, *Enneads*, 4.4.26–44; Starhawk, 1999: 155). According to our metaphysics (Sections 2 and 3), it utilizes the entanglements among eidolons. Since lower magic emerges from the entanglements among natural powers, it works within the natural constraints set by those entanglements. All agency in our universe is constrained by its laws of nature (Section 3.6). Thus lower magic does not (and cannot) violate the laws of nature (Starhawk, 1999: 159; Crowley, 2001: 76; Cunningham, 2004: 6; Alexander, 2014: 10; Beckett, 2017: 192–196). Of course, if our universe has a branching space-time, then the laws of nature usually permit an action to have many possible outcomes. Lower magic works within the constraints set by natural indeterminism. Nevertheless, lower magic only makes small changes, which often which often fail to produce the intended outcomes (Starhawk, 1999: 139; Crowley, 2001: 76; Cantrell, 2001: 162; Beckett, 2017: 192–201). If lower magic were reliably effective, then there would be scientific evidence for its effectiveness. Yet no such evidence exists (Beckett, 2017: 32; Sebastiani, 2020: 60). If lower magic were reliably effective, magicians would have exceptional (and noticeable) good luck. They would be conspicuously wealthy, healthy, and so on. They are not. Consequently, while lower magic may work in particular cases, it does not work reliably.

5.3 High Magic and Authenticity

Although the lower magic focuses on achieving mundane results, the *higher or greater magic* focuses on self-improvement. High magic involves "working your will to find your purpose in life and align with your higher self" (Sabin, 2011: 18). Or it involves aligning your consciousness with your body and the earth (Wildermuth, 2021: 151–169). High magic teaches us how to achieve self-realization and to act authentically. According to surveys done by Ruickbie

[33] While some Pagans say magic involves channeling spiritual forces (Crowley, 2001: ch. 4; Sebastiani, 2020: 60, 96), I am not aware of any who say it involves commanding supernatural persons.

(2004: ch. 9), Pagans mostly do magic for the sake of self-development. Thus most Pagan magic skews away from low magic to high magic. By focusing on self-realization, high magic is more spiritual (Parsons, 2022; Sonnex et al., 2022).

High magic teaches you how to exercise your true will (Starhawk, 1999: 137–139; Crowley, 2001: 56; Sabin, 2011: 18, 31, 196). When Crowley says that magic causes change in conformity with *will*, he means your *true will* (Sabin, 2011: 35–37; Alexander, 2014: 23, 180; Beckett, 2017: 190–191). True will contrasts with *want*, *wish* and *whim*. Sabin says your true will "is the force that drives you to your ultimate spiritual goal. It transcends want" (2011: 36). True will requires self-knowledge. Consistent with Pagan virtue ethics, truly willing some goal requires virtue. True will excludes self-centered wishes, and it transcends any egotistical will to power (Sylvan, 2012: 15). True will is authentic agency. The purpose of doing high magic is to learn to act with authenticity.

High magic teaches you to exercise personal agency. On this point, spells contrast with prayers (Sylvan, 2012: 33; Sebastiani, 2020: 102). In prayer, you ask a powerful divine agent to do something for you; in magic, you exercise your own power for yourself. Even if your magical power comes from the earth, or from some deity, you are the one who is raising it, shaping it, and projecting it towards your goal. Thus *high magic teaches you how to exercise the power you do have or can access, not how to acquire power you can't have or can't access* (Beckett, 2017: 200–201). Since humans are relatively small agents, magic teaches humility. Magic teaches that "if we can't fix the problems, we can live virtuously and valiantly in spite of them" (Beckett, 2017: 198).

High magic teaches you to maximize mundane action. High magic affirms the Pagan thesis that nature is a system of reciprocal relations. Reciprocity requires equal exchanges. If you want money, you generally have to earn it (Beckett, 2017: 201); it is rarely sufficient to light a green candle and chant a few words (contra Cunningham, 2004: 23–24). Likewise, if you want health, you have to earn it through disciplined living. *High magic insists on doing the reciprocal work needed to accomplish your goals* (Crowley, 2001: 80–81; Lafayllve, 2013: 128–129; Alexander, 2014: 225; Beckett, 2017: 196; Murphy-Hiscock, 2017: 24). You must exercise your agency. As Starhawk says, "A job spell is useless unless you also go out and look for a job. A healing spell is no substitute for medical care" (1999: 140). Beckett says, "Magic opens doors, and magic moves the odds in your favor, but magic won't do the work for you. What is your will?" (2017: 202). Here high magic helps you to resolve conflicts among your competing subwills (Beckett, 2017:

193–194), so that you can express a more coherent and therefore more effective agency.

High magic teaches you to align your will with the deities. Cunningham says, "magic is a process in which Wiccans work in harmony with the universal power source that we envision as the Goddess and God" (2004: 22). Sabin says, "When you act in accordance with your true will, you are in harmony with deity" (2011: 36). *High magic teaches you to align your will with the greatest good.* Vivianne Crowley says, "magic must be done in accordance with a greater scheme of things than one individual viewpoint" (2001: 90).[34] She says magic involves "harmonizing our intentions with the greater good" (2001: 134). And Cunningham says practicing magic requires affirming that your "future actions will be in accord with higher ideals and goals" beyond your self (2004: 6). Alexander advises witches to end their spells with "This is now accomplished in harmony with Divine Will, my own true will, and with good to all" (2014: 180, 190, 243).

High magic teaches you to take responsibility for your actions. Many Pagans stress that training in magic is training in personal responsibility (Cunningham, 2004: 6; Beckett, 2017: 197–200). Thus Carr-Gomm says, "the practice of magic [is] a conscious attempt to assume responsibility for our thoughts, words, and deeds" (2006: 54–55). Magic requires strength and clarity of will. It requires self-determination and self-control. Paganism usually advocates virtue ethics, and *high magic requires all the virtues*. It requires virtuous sovereignty. For instance, you cannot exercise your true will if you lie to yourself or to others; hence magic requires honesty (Starhawk, 1999: 138). You cannot exercise any will at all if you cannot keep your promises or honor your commitments. Hence magic requires the virtue of keeping promises (Starhawk, 1999: 138).

The main thesis of high magic is that the practice of high spellcasting causes your will to converge to your true will. As you practice high spellcasting, you get better and better at aligning your will with your true will. As you improve, you more habitually achieve this alignment. Thus the practice of high magic causes character changes which manifest in behavioral changes. It changes the quality of your agency in ways that make it more authentic. Greater authenticity entails that you understand your own strengths and weaknesses more accurately, so that you get better at setting more realistic goals, which you are more likely to achieve. Acting with greater authenticity entails that you act more carefully, more deliberately, more coherently, and more persistently. You cope better with adversity; you become more adaptive, more willing to experiment. For the high

[34] See Hanegraaff (1996: 90).

magician, to say that magic works means that it helps you act more authentically and effectively. Yet greater authenticity has positive practical consequences: high magic sharpens your agency in ways which increase the probability that you will achieve your goals. As high magicians become more adept, their wills become closer to their true wills. Hence they need to practice magic less and less (Crowley, 2001: 81; Sylvan, 2012: 15).

5.4 Spellcasting and Visualization

Magic, whether high or low, involves spellcasting, that is, casting spells. Spells are scripted procedures in which the caster manipulates symbols. These may be words, sounds, pictures, and small natural objects (stones, leaves, bones, and so on). Pagans sometimes find these objects during their immersive nature exercises. Starhawk says that "To cast a spell is to project energy through a symbol" (1999: 137). The scripts for spells resemble recipes for cooking, scripts for dramatic plays, and computer programs.

Spellcasting usually occurs within a ritual context. Sabin says, "A basic spell format is to create ritual space, state your intent, visualize your goal, raise energy, send the energy to your goal, ground the extra energy, and close the ritual" (2011: 197). Spellcasting usually involves *visualization*. Ancient Pagans like Plotinus have many visualization exercises (*Enneads*, 5.1.2.1–23, 5.8.9.1–30, 6.4.7.22–47, 6.7.15.25–33). Modern Neoplatonists continue this tradition (MacLennan, 2013: chs. 2 & 8). Since Wicca and witchcraft have roots in Neoplatonism, they have elaborate visualization exercises (e.g. Starhawk, 1999; Crowley, 2001; Cunningham, 2004: ch. 10; Sabin, 2011: ch. 3; Sylvan, 2012: 82–84; Roderick, 2021: 184).[35] Visualization projects images into the external world; it is a kind of willful semi-hallucination. It does not involve producing images in your head or with your eyes closed. For example, get an empty coffee cup, and, with your eyes wide open, visualize it as filled with coffee. *See* the coffee in the cup. Focus on its color, its texture, its reflectivity, and its motion. During visualization, you willfully project visualized energy from your body into your visualized scene.

According to the metaphysics of eidolons in Sections 2 and 3, willful visualization activates eidolons. Your empty coffee cup strongly instantiates the eidolon *empty-cup*. Likewise, it weakly instantiates the eidolon *full-cup*. The eidolons full-cup and empty-cup compete. When your cup is empty, the eidolon empty-cup has overpowered the eidolon full-cup. But the full-cup eidolon still has its intentionality, which aims at its strong manifestation; it still strives to be strongly

[35] Visualization also occurs in Druidry (Byghan, 2018: ch. 11). And in Asatru. Lafayllve gives exercises for visualizing the sun and the world tree Yggdrasil (2013: 18, 98–99). But it is discussed less frequently in these traditions.

instantiated in your cup. If you willfully visualize your cup as filled with coffee, then the full-cup eidolon becomes instantiated in your brain, and its intentionality becomes part of your intentionality (which wills that your cup is full). And, if you will that your cup is full, then the intentionality in your brain amplifies the intentionality of the full-cup eidolon in your brain; it eidetically energizes the full-cup eidolon in your brain. But your brain and your coffee cup eidetically overlap (Batty, 2023: 202): the full-cup eidolon which gains eidetic energy in your brain is also instantiated in your cup, and it gains eidetic energy in the cup.

The metaphysics of eidolons asserts that *if any brain willfully visualizes some eidolon, then that brain causes that eidolon to gain some extra eidetic energy (Isness) towards producing a strong self-instance in the external context specified by that vision.* Accordingly, eidetic energy (Isness) flows from your brain into the full-cup instance in your brain, and thus flows equally into the full-cup instance in the cup. Hence the instance of full-cup at your coffee cup gains greater eidetic energy. *If any eidolon gains greater energy in some context, then it strives more intensely to be strongly instantiated there*. So the eidolon full-cup strives more intensely to be strongly instantiated in your coffee cup. That spacetime region strives more intensely to contain coffee. *But if any eidolon strives more intensely to have a strong self-instance at some region, then it becomes more probable that it does have a strong self-instance there.* By willfully visualizing your cup as filled with coffee, it becomes more probable that it will contain coffee. This need not mean your visualization will cause you to put some coffee into the cup. Somebody else might spontaneously and unexpectedly come by to fill your cup. Or your cup might get filled in some way which is exceptional yet within physical constraints.

On this view, visualization causally increases the probability that the events it depicts will occur. According to the metaphysics of eidolons, that increase in probability is objective, and visualization physically changes our universe. On the one hand, those who practice low magic are deeply interested in these changes. For the low magician, visualization works if and only if the cup gets filled. The low magician is mainly interested in the cup. Of course, its filling respects natural laws. Perhaps somebody unexpectedly comes by to fill it. Here the low magician wonders whether this unexpected event confirms that the visualization worked, or whether it was merely coincidence.

On the other hand, those who practice high magic have little primary interest in the instrumental outcome of the spell. Whether or not your cup gets filled is mainly incidental. The true purpose of visualization is to train your mind to see your possible futures more clearly so you can learn to evaluate their alignments with your true will. For the high magician, to say visualization works means that it helps you to exercise your true will. The high magician stresses that *your true will is your strongest intentionality;* if filling the cup is not your true will, your visualization won't add much power to the eidolons. The success of high visualization does not require your cup to get filled; it requires you to learn something about your authentic agency. And, if somebody unexpectedly does comes by to fill your cup, the high magician need not marvel or rejoice much in this mundane event. But the high magician does become alert to the entanglement of some new person in their life. The high magician is also alert to the thesis that low magic does little more than produce an illusion of control (Langer, 1975). However, for the high magician, that illusion is a valuable cognitive scaffold which can be used in the construction of authentic agency. To cast a high spell is to create a work of performance art. Again pointing to Noe (2018), spells are strange tools which help us to develop our true wills.

5.5 Spells in Low and High Magic

Here is a spell from Sabin which probably lies closer to low magic. It aims at protecting your house (2011: 210–213). It involves creating a "witch bottle." While the spell is situated in a larger ritual context, here I focus on the construction of the bottle. You gather these props: a small bottle with a lid or cork, some sharp objects like nails or tacks, some black strings, some red wine, and a black candle. The colors are meaningful symbols: red indicates protective aggression, while black indicates banishing. Now the spell begins. Drop the sharp objects into the bottle, while visualizing "negative energy being repelled from your home". Drop some strings into the bottle, while visualizing "negative energy being bound up in the threads". Pour the wine into the bottle, while visualizing it as "washing away all the negative stuff that might approach your home". To complete the spell, close the bottle with its lid or cork and seal it with black wax to bind all negativities in the bottle. After the wax cools, bury the bottle in your front yard and "visualize it sending out an energetic barrier that repels harmful things." Sabin offers short incantations to perform during each action. A witch bottle weakly instantiates an eidolon of domestic protection (an eidolon which is more strongly instantiated in guard dogs, fences, and so on). By making the witch bottle, you aim to shift energy from your brain into that eidolon, making it more competitive. As low magic, this spell works as long as your home remains safe and secure; it fails if your home gets violated or damaged. As described by Sabin, this spell has little to do with exercising your true will. But it could become part of a higher magical practice. The buried bottle could persistently remind you of the vulnerability of your home; it might motivate you to take mundane steps to protect it; it might encourage you to think about how to best cope with its damage or destruction. This leads into the Stoic technique of visualizing misfortunes in advance (Pigliucci, 2017: 151–152).

Here is a spell which pretty clearly exemplifies high magic. It was cast by a young woman named Scarlett (Rountree, 2002). Scarlett believes she is stuck in her childhood, and she seeks to transform herself into an adult. The goal of her spell is self-realization. She casts a spell whose goal is her mature self:

> She showed us a picture she had drawn of her family with herself as a little, dirty girl at the end of a family of five. She ripped up this picture and put it into a box through a slot in the top, symbolically destroying this image of her place in the family. She then produced a fragment of an old child's garment, telling us that this was a symbol of her childhood. . . . The clothing fragment was put into the box with the ripped-up picture. Scarlett said she had a lot of childish habits which she wanted to leave behind. . . . She scattered dead leaves representing the habits in the center of the circle and trampled them. She then announced her decision to wear clean, bright clothes and pulled a purple silk scarf out through the slot in the box. She produced some new patent leather shoes bought that day as a gift to herself, and put them on along with the scarf. Finally, she lit a very tall red candle to symbolize the bold adult status she was choosing to claim. (Rountree, 2002: 54)

The props in Scarlett's spell weakly instantiate eidolons corresponding to her childhood and to her mature adult self. Her acts decrease the energies of the childhood eidolons and increase the energies of the adulthood eidolons. Her entire spell instantiates the process-eidolon of maturing into a self-directing adult. By de-energizing the childhood eidolons, and energizing the adulthood eidolons, her spellcasting makes the adulthood eidolons objectively more powerful in their competitions with the childhood eidolons, and thereby makes them objectively more likely to grow stronger in Scarlett's future.

This spell pretty clearly aims to help Scarlett realize her authentic self, and to thereby exercise her true will. It maps out a class of desired possible futures using visible symbols, which can help Scarlett keep those futures fixed vividly in her mind. Carruthers (2015) argues that we cannot think without sensory contents. But our futures are so vague that our unaided minds usually cannot equip them with any sensory contents. High magic produces visible maps of future projects. And Scarlett's spell required some effort to produce and was publicly performed. It is a costly social signal of her commitment to realizing her mature self. Scarlett herself went on to complete a degree in fine arts. Here the low magician will say the spell worked in the low sense: it energized a structure of eidolons, so that they prevailed against their competitors to become strongly instantiated in Scarlett's future. The high magician will say the spell worked in the high sense, and the high magician can agree that greater eidetic energies helped it to work in the high sense. To some degree, high magic incorporates low magic. But the high magician says that the external eidetic changes caused by the spell were probably only small and transient. The primary effect of the spell was to change the power relations of the eidolons in Scarlett's brain. The spell worked in the high sense because it helped Scarlett to exercise her true will over many years. It helped her become an authentic agent.

6 Ethics

6.1 Ethics in the Network

According to the Pagan metaphysics sketched in Sections 2 and 3, Nature is a network of interacting nodes, each of which is animated by an eidolon. Every node essentially contains a (local) law within itself.[36] Since these nodes are animated, these laws drive or *compel* the nodes to act. Since its law is essential to itself, the node is bound to that law as it is bound to its own being and that bond therefore has *normative force* for the node (Christensen, 2012). If some node contains a law which compels it to act, then it governs itself according to that law, and the compelling force of the law is a command which comes from its essence, that is, from its nature. Its own nature commands it to act in certain ways. The node has a *duty to itself* to obey its law, to act as its law commands. Animated by its own law, every node in Nature is an *agent* (Ellis, 2014: 3, 31).[37] Rivers and mountains and planets are agents; bacteria, plants, fungi, and animals are agents.

On the one hand, as a node, every agent exists in and for itself; it has its own essential law. Since it is governed by its law, it has *autonomy*. Its autonomy entails that it has the duty of self-determination or self-governance; it has the duty to itself to unfold its futurity in accordance with its own law. Duties generally entail *rights*. The duty of self-determination entails the right of self-determination. This right is the *wildness*, *freedom*, or *sovereignty* of the agent. On the other hand, as a node in a network, every agent is bound to other agents by its relations to them and theirs to it. Its bonds with other agents define its *boundary*. Thus any agent in a network has *bounded sovereignty*. Its boundary defines the range in which it can *ethically* exercise its sovereignty. Within its boundary, an agent has rights, its actions are right or appropriate, and it acts ethically; beyond its boundary, it has no rights, its acts are wrong or

[36] Jamison (2010) and York (2015) provide surveys of Pagan ethics.

[37] This agency is not Kantian; it is the agency of located eidolons. Eidolons are powerful self-regulating natures.

inappropriate, and it acts unethically. Granted that Pagan metaphysics entails bounded sovereignty, it follows that Pagan ethics will tend towards *deontology* (stressing duties and rights). And, granted that virtues are habitual dispositions which help agents do their duties, Pagans will endorse *virtue ethics*.

When any agent is bound to another, it becomes bound to itself through that other, so its duty to itself passes through that other, and it becomes a duty to that other. But the bonds in Nature are symmetrical: if any agent in Nature is bound to any other agent, then that other agent is also bound to it. The duties of agents thus become entangled, so that the duties of an agent to itself give rise to its duties to others. Wildermuth says Pagans see "everything as mutual relation and obligation" (2021: 101).[38] This symmetry is the basis for ethical *reciprocity*. Greer says that since all beings "share in a network of reciprocal relationships of exchange, every being is connected to every other being in a closely woven fabric of reciprocity" (2023: 102). Reciprocity is central to Pagan ethics (Greer, 2023: ch. 8). Reciprocity is expressed in the well-known maxim that you reap what you sow. And reciprocity grounds the golden rule: do unto others as you would have them do unto you. Reciprocity regulates relations between all organisms, including between humans and gods (Beckett, 2017: 43–44; Greer, 2023: ch. 8), humans and humans, humans and nonhuman organisms, and nonhuman organisms and each other.

Reciprocity plays a central role in Pagan ethical thinking. For Wiccans, reciprocity is codified in the longer version of the *Wiccan Rede*, a poem which expresses some Wiccan ethical principles (Cantrell, 2001: ch. 2; Roderick, 2005: 259–260; Sabin, 2011: ch. 2; Sylvan, 2012: ch. 3). One of these is the *law of return*: "What ye send out, comes back to thee" (Batty, 2023: 111). The return is symmetrical: when you do good, you receive good; when you do evil, you receive evil. Reciprocity plays a central role in Druidism (Carr-Gomm, 2006: ch.7; Billington, 2011: 93–96, 228, 261, 281; Byghan, 2018: ch. 2). Reciprocity plays a central role in Asatru (Lafayllve, 2013: 149–150). Nordvig says, "The whole world is reciprocal: *Do ut des* – give to receive" (2020: 72). Of course, you might object that the evidence runs counter to this reciprocity: good people often have lives with horrific bad luck, while evil-doers get blessing after blessing. Here Pagans can reply that karmic laws extend reciprocity beyond our present lives.

6.2 Ethics for All Organisms

Although Pagan ethics includes relations between nonliving things, and between living and nonliving things, most Pagan ethical thinking focuses on living things. So I will focus on that here. Since the essential laws of organisms

[38] Contra Harvey (2006), all things, whether persons or not, are bound into networks of mutual obligation.

are shaped by evolution, evolution gives every organism its basic duties to itself. These are its inherited obligations (Beckett, 2017: 178). Every organism has the general duty to itself to pursue its evolved way of life. This is its *duty to flourish*. Ultimately, this is its duty to act in accordance with its true will. More biologically, this general duty usually (but not always) breaks down into at least two more specific duties. Every organism has the *duty to grow* from its original form (spore, seed, zygote) to its optimal or mature form. And it has the *duty to reproduce* and to raise its offspring until they are independent. These duties entail that every organism has the *duty to survive* for an optimal length of time defined by its evolved nature. Of course, these duties to self are sometimes overridden by duties to others. Among the social insects, most do not reproduce. Among the social insects, and among humans, soldiers may sacrifice their lives for the greater good of their societies.

The duty to flourish entails two outward-facing duties. The first outward-facing duty is an *offensive duty*, namely, the *duty of sustenance.* This duty states that, every organism, driven by its own evolved law of self-determination, has the duty take exactly what it needs to flourish from other organisms and its environment. It has the duty to take all and only what it needs; it has the duty to take neither less nor more than it needs. It has the duty to take air, water, food, shelter, and so on. The second outward-facing duty is a *defensive duty*, namely, the *duty of self-defense.* It states that every organism has the duty prevent others from taking anything that compromises its sovereignty. These duties entail rights: every organism has the *right to sustenance* and the *right of self-defense.*

Among organisms, the difference between acting within or beyond rights enters into many morally significant biological distinctions. An organism is *hurt* when it is biologically damaged in any way, but an organism is only *harmed* when it is hurt by some wrong action of another organism. That is, *harming is wrongful hurting.* Since being damaged is correlated with suffering in organisms, being hurt is usually correlated with suffering. Animals with nervous systems experience suffering as pain, but plants also experience suffering as meaningful distress mediated by specialized signals. To cause suffering is to cause hurt, but it need not cause harm. Analogously, an organism is *killed* when its life is brought to an end, but it is only *murdered* when it is killed by the wrong action of another organism. Thus murdering is wrongful killing.

Bounded sovereignty entails that all organisms are free to act within their rights. This freedom is expressed in short Wiccan Rede (which is often taken to be the Rede itself). The (short) Rede says: *if you harm none, do what you will.* This is usually interpreted as: as long as you are doing no harm, then do what you will. But doing no harm is equivalent to acting within your rights.

Therefore, the Rede says, as long as you act within your rights, do what you will. Your will is not merely what you want; the Rede does not say, do what you wish or do what you whim. Granted that the Rede is at least partly inspired by Crowley's notion of true will (Section 5.2), your will is your true will. Your true will comes from your autonomy, from your law of self-determination. Your true will is theurgical: it maximizes the probability of achieving your ideals; but this requires maximizing your flourishing. Therefore, the Rede says, as long as you act within your rights, maximize your flourishing. Yet the Rede is silent about actions that cause harm. It does not say, if *and only if* it harms none, do what you will. But here the law of return comes into play: if you act beyond your rights, you get the consequences.

As organisms evolve, they become entangled. They can provide resources for each other. Economic relations emerge between organisms. Economic relations involve exchanges of resources and services. Since the organisms in these economic relations have the rights of sustenance and self-defense, those rights appear in these economic relations. If one organism can supply resources to another, then they become related as producer and consumer. The right of sustenance entails that the consumer has a right to take those resources from the producer. The right of self-defense entails that the producer has the right to prevent the consumer from taking too much. Evolution tunes these economic relations into cooperative or competitive relations. Cooperative relations involve nondestructive exchanges of resources or services. The flower provides sustenance (nectar and pollen) for the bee; the bee provides the service of pollinating the flower. In lichens, fungi and algae provide services for each other to flourish.

6.3 Organisms Compete

Competitive relations involve destructive exchanges of resources or services. In competitive relations, the organisms are negatively entangled: the good of the one negates the good of the other. As they pursue their goods, their goods conflict. Hence their duties and their rights conflict. The most common type of competitive relation is *predation*. While there are many definitions of predation, here I define predation generally: it occurs when one organism (the predator) eats all or part of any other organism (the prey). Thus animals or plants eating animals (carnivory) is predation; animals eating plants is predation (herbivory). Likewise predation includes parasitism, in which the predator (the parasite) lives inside of its prey (the host) and usually allows it to live.

Predation is common in our earthly biosphere. Bacteria and fungi consume the flesh of living organisms (both plants and animals). Amoeba are predators which eat bacteria. Paramecia prey on smaller single-celled organisms. Carnivorous plants eat insects, reptiles, and mammals. Predation is very common among animals: insects, arthropods, birds, reptiles, and mammals are all predators. Some animal predators eat plankton, plants, or fungi; others eat other animals. Although viruses might not be alive, they display a kind of predation when they hijack the genetic machinery in cells to reproduce. Parasitism (which is a kind of predation) is also very common in our earthly biosphere. Plants and animals are parasitized by bacteria, protists, fungi, insects, worms, and so on.

Pagans recognize that life eats life (Starhawk, 1999: 36; Roderick, 2005: 133; Beckett, 2017: 174; Byghan, 2018: 32; Wildermuth, 2021: 94–97). If predation is wrong, then most of life is essentially doing wrong and is therefore evil. But if most of life is evil, then life is not sacred. Since Pagans think life is sacred, they must infer that life is not evil, and that predation is not evil. Hence many Pagans ethically defend predation. Wildermuth outlines an ecological ethics, including a defense of animal predation (2021: 85–106). He says predation provides a service to prey species by enhancing their fitnesses (2021: 96). Roderick (2005: 133–134) views predation from a "deity perspective." The theophany of Demeter (all the plants) nourishes that of Artemis (all the animals); the theophany of Artemis grooms that of Demeter. The theophany of Chloris (goddess of flowers) nourishes that of Aristaeus (god of bees), while Aristaeus fertilizes Chloris. These astral bodies provide necessary ecological services for each other and are not harmed. While these are intriguing suggestions, resolving this issue requires more detailed work.

Predation pits the right to sustenance of the predator against the right to flourish of the prey. According to the theory of bounded sovereignty, the predator has the right to take exactly what it needs from its prey, and the prey has the right to defend itself against the predator. Some Pagans explicitly recognize these rights. Foxes sometimes eat the eggs of ducks. Byghan says the fox has the right to take the duck's eggs and the duck has the right to attack the fox (2018: 32). As another example, hawks have the right to hunt, attack, eat, and kill squirrels. Likewise, squirrels have the right to defend themselves by escaping. But reciprocity further entails that squirrels have the right to defend themselves by attacking hawks (squirrels have sharp teeth, which can sever the tendons in the legs of hawks, causing them to release the squirrels and later to die). And parasites have the right to infect their hosts. Viruses, bacteria, fungi, and protists have the right to infect their hosts; their hosts have the right to use their immune systems against them. Both predator and prey have rights; sometimes they act within them, sometimes they do not.

When two organisms conflict, and each is within its rights, no wrong is done. While the fox is taking from the duck, the fox is not taking wrongfully, so the fox is not stealing. Or return to the case of the hawk and the squirrel. They come into conflict when their bodies collide. If the hawk captures and eats the squirrel, then the right of the hawk prevails over the right of the squirrel. Since the hawk acts within its rights, it does no wrong. Although it *hurts* the squirrel (causing it pain and suffering), it does not hurt it wrongly; therefore, it does not *harm* the squirrel. Although it *kills* the squirrel, it does not kill it wrongly; therefore, it does not *murder* the squirrel. Conversely, if the squirrel severs a tendon in the hawk's leg, so it can no longer hunt, and it starves to death, then the squirrel acts within its rights and does no wrong. The squirrel has fatally hurt the hawk, but has neither harmed nor murdered it. The same holds true if the squirrel merely escapes, so that the hawk is weakened by hunger, and therefore starves to death.

When conflicting rights are ethically resolved, justice is done, and the outcome is just. According to the theory of bounded sovereignty, when two conflicting organisms are both acting within their rights, their conflict is ethical, and the outcome is just. The conflict between hawk and squirrel is just and so is the outcome. If the squirrel is eaten and killed, that is just; if the hawk is injured and starves to death, that is just. But justice entails that each party gets what it deserves. Whatever happens in the conflict between hawk and squirrel, each party gets what it deserves. If the squirrel is eaten and killed, then it deserved to suffer and die; if the hawk is fatally injured, then it deserved to suffer and die.

The theory of bounded sovereignty entails that, far from being amoral or immoral, evolution finely tunes organisms for justice towards each other. Of course, this does not entail that humans should act like hawks, or wolves, or like other animals. The law of self-determination entails that hawks should act like hawks, and humans should act like humans. Humans are *rational social animals;* hawks and squirrels are not. Doctrines like *social Darwinism* portray humans as if we were nonhuman animals, lacking both rationality and rational sociality. Such doctrines pervert human nature. Humans place bonds on each other which hawks and squirrels do not place on each other.

When two organisms conflict, and either is not within its rights, then at least one of them does wrong, and the conflict is unjust on at least one side. Each organism that is not within its rights is acting unjustly, and it is doing wrong. It is harming and perhaps murdering the other organism. If a cat kills more birds than it needs to eat, then it is acting beyond its right to sustenance; since it is acting in excess of its right, its action is wrong, and its killing is murdering. Conversely, if a bird does not fully strive to defend itself against a predator, its failure to exercise its right of self-defense is wrong.

By consuming nutrients and energies, organisms grow. Every organism has the duty (hence the right) to grow to its optimum (mature) size. But it has no right to grow beyond that. Likewise, every species has the right to grow to its optimum (mature) size. The size of the species is the total region occupied by its member organisms. A species grows to its optimum (mature) size by filling its ecological niches in an optimal way. But a species has no right to grow beyond its optimal size. If any organism or species grows beyond its optimal size, then that excess growth is wrong. It acts unjustly. It has no right to sustenance beyond its optimal size. Hence any organism or species which seeks nutrition (or other resources) to grow beyond its optimal size is acting unjustly. Its predatory acts are wrong; it is harming and murdering other organisms. Here it seems plausible that an immoral population size is an unsustainable population size.

For example, in the late 1900s, in Yellowstone, the elk population soared far beyond its optimal size for that bioregion. The excessive elk population wrongly destroyed much vegetation; that immoral overgrazing caused further immoral ecological degradation. This excess was harmful to the elk as well. After wolves were reintroduced in the 1990s, those wolves rightfully killed those excess elk, thereby rightfully enabling the vegetation and the elk themselves to flourish (Boyce, 2018). As another example, many Pagans argue that humans (and human patterns of consumption) have expanded far beyond their optimal size for the earth. Hopefully, we will be able to ethically reduce our population size and consumption patterns to optimal levels.

6.4 Organisms Cooperate

The theory of bounded sovereignty includes all the ways that organisms at all levels of complexity bind themselves to each other by cooperative relations, thus forming cooperative networks. Say these cooperative networks are *federations* composed of *individuals*. There are three main types of federations: cells bond into loose societies (like bacterial biofilms); cells fuse into multi-cellular organisms (like sponges or humans); organisms bond into societies (like mutualisms, flocks, or packs). My discussion of the moral aspects of cooperation is severely compressed due to space constraints. For a far more detailed and nuanced presentation, see Steinhart (2022: chs. 6 & 7).

As these federations evolved, a general system of moral properties, relations, and behaviors evolved within them. I will refer to this moral system as the *moral pattern*, which I outline here. To cooperate, these individuals must enter into a *social contract*, which constrains them to behave according to *norms*. They must *altruistically sacrifice* their *rights* for the greater good of the federation. For example, the cells that form multi-cellular organisms muss sacrifice two core cellular rights: the right to eat other cells, and the right to self-reproduce. Within any federation, each individual *prohibits* itself from pursuing these *forbidden* options. Conversely, each individual must *obligate* itself to share resources with its neighbors. It *promises* to share resources with others. Norms of *reciprocity* emerge to regulate this sharing. The main reciprocity norm is the *golden rule*, that is, the *tit-for-tat interaction strategy* in game theory (Axelrod, 1984).

As individuals fuse into a federation, they typically specialize into distinctive functional *roles*. Plotinus offered an early organizational account of functions (*Enneads*, 3.3.1, 6.8.14–17), which repeats in modern biology (Christensen & Bickhard, 2002). Ancient Pagans like Plotinus and Epictetus argued that functional roles confer *duties*, which individuals *ought* to perform within the federation. The notion that roles confer duties also reoccurs in modern biology (Moreno & Mossio, 2015). Within the federation, *cheaters* may emerge which *steal* social *benefits* without paying social *costs*. Mechanisms of *altruistic punishment* emerge in the federation to inhibit or eliminate such cheaters (Kiers & Denison, 2008; Mills & Cote, 2010). More generally, the *categorical imperative* emerges within federations, acting like a *ratchet* which prevents the society of cooperators from backsliding to lower complexity (Libby & Ratcliff, 2014).

All these moral features appear, for example, when single-celled social amoebas swarm together to form a multi-cellular federation called a slug (Li & Purugganan, 2011; Ostrowski, 2019). All these moral features appear as individual cells form multi-cellular organisms and as colonies of specialized cells form organs within complex organisms. They appear in biological mutualisms, in which individuals from many species form an economic federation. They appear as nitrogen-fixing microbes form federations with carbon-generating plants (Kiers & Denison, 2008; Leigh, 2010). They appear in the mutualism of flowering plants and their insect pollinators (Ketcham, 2020). Just as cells merge into organisms, so social insects merge into super-organisms. Specialized groups of insects act like organs in those super-organisms (Holldobler & Wilson, 2009). All the moral features emerge in these super-organisms (Arnhart, 1998: ch. 3).

This moral pattern emerges as individual nonhuman animals merge into nonhuman animal federations (Bekoff & Pierce 2009; Rowlands, 2012). Just a few examples of the moral pattern in nonhuman animals' societies are listed here. The moral pattern emerges in societies of corvids (Clayton & Emery 2007; Boucherie et al. 2019). It emerges in societies of canids (Pierce & Bekoff 2012). Likewise many similar types of moral norms are found in societies of cetaceans (Vincent et al., 2019). Moral norms are found in societies of chimpanzees (Pierce & Bekoff, 2012; Vincent et al., 2019; Fitzpatrick, 2020). Since humans are organisms, the general moral pattern emerges in human societies too, and Pagans can turn to evolutionary accounts of human morality (e.g. Joyce, 2006; Tomasello, 2016).

6.5 Human Ethics

Since Pagan ethics emerges from the metaphysics of Nature as a relational network of agents with bounded sovereignty, Pagan ethics will be holistic and relational. At the most basic level, Paganism defines right and wrong in terms of networks: an action is right when it tends to preserve or enhance the positive values of the natural network; it is wrong otherwise. Some of these positivities were discussed in Section 2.4. Perhaps the most general positivity of networks is just complexity, where the complexity of a network is proportional to the diversity of its nodes and the diversity of their connections. Properties like beauty and harmony are proxies for complexity and network positivity. Of course, the natural network includes all things on earth, whether living or not; yet most Pagan ethics focuses on the network of living things, the ecological web of life. Hence Pagans will tend to endorse Leopold's *land ethic*: an action "is right when it tends to preserve the integrity, stability, and beauty of the biotic community. It is wrong when it tends otherwise" (1949: 224–225). Many Pagans do endorse something like this land ethic (Starhawk, 1999: 34–35; Crowley, 2001: ch. 3; Beckett, 2017: ch. 3; Byghan, 2018: ch. 2; Wildermuth, 2021: 85–106; Batty, 2023: 145–146; Greer, 2023: 102).

General principles involving networks are usually far too abstract to enter into the everyday lives of Pagans. Pagans need to reason from their general principles to the specifics that work in everyday situations. Wiccans tend to derive their specific ethical principles by applying the Wiccan Rede to specific situations. Other Pagans give lists of specific moral values and moral codes to serve those values (Carr-Gomm, 2006: 57; Byghan, 2018: ch. 2; Nordvig, 2020: ch. 3). Many Pagans develop detailed virtue ethics (Billington, 2011: 192–195; Sylvan, 2012: 49–61; Lafayllve, 2013: ch. 12; Nordvig, 2020: ch. 3; Sebastiani, 2020: 56–59; Paxson, 2021: 140–144). Unfortunately, space does not permit me to present these moral codes in detail.

Obviously, there are many ways to go from general principles to specific principles. And, since Pagans tend to highly value diversity and independence, they in fact differ on many ethical issues. Pagans have plenty of disagreements about sex, diet, and other aspects of human life. Pagans occupy pretty much every position on the political spectrum from far left to far right. However, some political positions are not consistent with the general principles of Pagan ethics. For example, some Pagans, particularly those in Germanic heathenry (the Odinists), are racists (Schnurbein, 2016). Fortunately, the vast majority of Pagans (including most Germanic heathens) emphatically reject this racism (see Paxson, 2021: ch. 5). General Pagan commitments to diversity, equality, and reciprocity entail that racism is not consistent with Pagan ethics (Strmiska,

2020). Here I will give several arguments against racism from general Pagan ethical principles.

The first argument comes from sovereignty. A deep Pagan ethical principle asserts that all beings have *equal sovereignty* (Sections 3.5, 4.2, 6.1). All humans are born with equal sovereignty. And all humans are born with differences in inherited characteristics (even if these are merely epigenetic). It follows that humans with different inherited characteristics share the same sovereignty. To deny them equal sovereignty based on their inherited characteristics violates a deep Pagan ethical principle. Since racism, and sexism, and many other forms of discrimination deny equal sovereignty based on inherited characteristics, those positions deeply oppose Pagan ethics.

The second argument comes from reciprocity. A deep Pagan ethical principle states that all things are bound to each other by *reciprocal obligations* (Sections 2.4, 6.1). Hence Pagan ethics affirms principles of reciprocity like the golden rule and the categorical imperative. Assuming that no human wants to be the victim of racism, the golden rule forbids every human from making others victims of racism. Kant's categorical imperative is even stronger. One very quick way to put it states that laws are moral if and only if they hold universally for all rational beings. But laws which discriminate against any subset of rational beings based on their inherited characteristics are by definition not universal. It follows that racism violates a deep Pagan ethical principle.

The third argument comes from the fact that Pagan ethics is *virtue ethics*. This is especially true for the Asatru (Lafayllve, 2013: ch. 12; Paxson, 2021: 140–144). The moral quality of a person is expressed through and only through the moral qualities (virtuous or vicious) of their deeds. The Asatru writer Smith says, "the measure of a person is in their deeds" (2019: 7). Lafayllve says, "Heathen ethical systems ... are based on the actions taken in the here and now" (2013: 146–147). Hence the only evidence acceptable for the moral evaluation of a person's character is the record of their deeds (Lafayllve, 2013: 62–63, 147–149; Smith, 2019: ch. 5). Clearly, inherited features are not deeds (they are part of your *orlog*) and are therefore useless for evaluating moral worth. Hence Smith says, "the inherent traits of race, gender, sexuality, national origin, physical or mental ability, are not and never should be used for assessing anyone's worth" (2019: 7).

7 Practices

7.1 Theosis and Theurgy

According to the archaic Pagan theology (Section 4.1), the deities are superbodies; that is, they are functionally superior versions of earthly organisms. Their divine bodies are animated by divine eidolons. Since every thing participates to some degree in every eidolon, including every divine eidolon, all humans participate weakly in the divine eidolons. It is plausible to say that *religious practices* are deliberate activities through which we strive to become maximally connected to the deities.

One way to make yourself maximally connected to some deity is via *theosis*. Theosis is the practice of deliberately making yourself as much like some deity as possible. Ancient Pagans advocated theosis. Plato often endorsed it (*Phaedrus*, 252 c-253 c; *Ion*, 533d; *Theaetetus*, 176a5-b2). Plotinus says our goal is to live "the life of the gods: for it is to them . . . that we are to be made like" (*Enneads*, 1.2.7.25–32). Beckett says that we ought to try to become gods (2017: 144–146). Through theosis, you try to make your body animated, as strongly as possible, by some divine eidolon. Of course, we cannot literally transform ourselves into deities; during all religious practices, humans remain humans. The most we can do is to virtually transform ourselves into deities by imitating or simulating them. We can become avatars or living statues of the deities. This is *ritual mimesis*.

Iamblichus argued that, to make ourselves more like the deities, we need ritual practices which involve bodily activity (*On the Mysteries*, 2.11). These practices were known as *theurgy* (Shaw, 2014). Theurgical rituals aim at theosis. Through theurgical rituals, Iamblichus says that a human can "assume the mantle of the gods" (*On the Mysteries*, 4.2). The purpose of theurgy, according to Shaw, "is not to escape from the body but to . . . allow the divine to take its seat in one's own body" (2015: 158). Thus "Deified theurgists do not escape from their bodies or from nature; they embrace both from a divine perspective" (2015: 159). Shaw says that, through theurgy, "the human being became transformed into a living icon of the god" (2013: 6714). To be an icon of something is to instantiate its eidolon as intensely as possible. A living icon is a living statue, an avatar. To theurgically instantiate a divine eidolon is to *channel* that eidolon or deity.

During any type of theurgy, your human eidolon shifts into an altered state which exceeds ordinary humanity in the direction of a deity. You become *transhuman*, that is, a human engaged in surpassing its own humanity. Thus you participate in the self-surpassivity of the One (i.e. Isness). Hence theurgy often involves *ecstasy*, that is, stepping outside of your humanity by simulating a deity. This is *edgework* (Lyng, 1990). You enter the liminal boundary between human and divine. To channel a deity in this way is to become a *wild human*. Arousing this wildness in the motions of your body, you more intensely participate in the wildness of the One. But wildness does not entail any loss of self-control; on the contrary, it requires superlative self-direction, the height of bounded sovereignty, divine autonomy, and the self-law of a deity. This wildness is often correlated with the altered state of consciousness known as *flow* (Csikszentmihalyi, 2002).

7.2 Some Types of Theurgy

A first type of theurgy involves *possession trances*. During a possession trance, a human becomes animated, ridden, or cognitively occupied by a divine eidolon. Possession trances occur in many types of Paganism (Starhawk, 1999: ch. 9; Sabin, 2011: ch. 4; Beckett, 2017: 267). In the Wiccan ritual of *drawing down the moon*, a human becomes possessed by the Wiccan Goddess; in *drawing down the sun*, they become possessed by the Wiccan God (Farrar & Farrar, 1981: 67–70, 296–297; Hill, 2020; Batty, 2023: 103). The practice of *seidr* in Asatru involves trance and may involve divine possession (Lafayllve, 2013: ch. 11; Paxson, 2021: ch. 9; Nordvig, 2020: ch. 6). Ecstatic dance can induce possession trances. One recent form of Western ecstatic dance occurs at festivals known as *raves*. Many raves involve Pagan religious elements (Sylvan, 2005) and are thus plausibly regarded as Pagan festivals. While dancing, ravers sometimes enter trances, in which they report channeling divine energies and deities (Sylvan, 2005: 88–93; Redfield, 2017: 71). However, eidolons are not immaterial minds, and your body in trance is not occupied by some alien nonphysical mind. During some possession trance, some divine eidolon becomes unusually intensely instantiated by your body. The-deity-in-your-body alters or reshapes your mentality into that unusual yet entirely human kind of mentality which is most appropriately associated with that divine eidolon.

A second type of theurgy involves channeling a deity by deliberately participating in some characteristic activity of that deity. Hence your body in motion more intensely instantiates the eidolon of that deity. You can channel Artemis by hunting with a weapon or a camera. You move with the virtues of a predator. You move carefully and mindfully, with deliberate and disciplined intention, based on extensive training and practice. You enact the virtues of stealth and agility. You can channel Hermes through endurance running. When your body religiously instantiates the divine eidolon of the transhuman runner, when you are possessed by the divine runner, you feel the *runner's high*.

A third type of theurgy is *shamanic*. It involves *shape-shifting*. Here a human channels the divine eidolons of other animals (see Lupa, 2021). Shape-shifting involves disciplined motions of the body. You channel the divine avian eidolon by acting like a bird. You can imitate birdsong. You can get into a hang glider or wingsuit and fly. You channel the divine fish eidolon by acting like a fish. You get into the water and swim in more than merely human ways. You put on a monofin, reshaping your feet into a fish tail. You use a snorkel or aqualung to remain underwater in some more than merely human way. You can channel the divine bat eidolon by navigating using echolocation. By performing these activities mindfully, that is, deliberately and skillfully, you virtually acquire the virtues of these divine animal eidolons. You acquire bird virtues, fish virtues, and bat virtues. Done in a way that engages divine eidolons, this shape-shifting is also edgework. It transforms your human eidolon into that of a wild human, a bird-human or fish-human. Shape-shifting includes the adoption of animal identities by the Otherkin (Laycock, 2012).

A fourth type of theurgy involves driving your body to the edge of human performance. Done deliberately and mindfully, with spiritual intention, you point your animality towards the superhuman animality of the divine bodies. This type of theurgy usually occurs in those *extreme sports* which involve religious engagement with earthly nature (Brymer & Gray, 2009). Pagans advocate immersion in earthly nature (Section 3.3), and extreme sports are extremely immersive. Religiously meaningful extreme sports include mountaineering (Stutfield, 1918; Driscoll & Atwood, 2020) and surfing (Taylor, 2007). These sports are examples of religious edgework; they push human bodies beyond the merely human into the transhuman. Participants in extreme sports channel the eidolons of transhuman animals, thereby participating in their transhuman virtues. Hiking the entire Appalachian trail (2190 miles) is an arduous spiritual pilgrimage (Redick, 2018).

Not all types of theurgy require ordeals. A fifth type of theurgy involves breath meditation. Breath meditation occurs in many types of Paganism (e.g. Lafayllve, 2013: 97–98, 142–143; Beckett, 2017: 133–134). Like Buddhist breath meditation, Pagan breath meditation often involves focusing your attention on your breathing. When your mind wanders, gently return your attention to the rhythmic process of inhaling and exhaling. Through breath meditation, you channel a very general, powerful, and deep eidolon, namely, the eidolon of cyclicality. Humans who practice breath meditation often declare that it induces an altered state of consciousness which seems superhuman, and which is therefore more divine. Simple practices done mindfully and with deliberate religious intention can channel deities. Domestic deities (like Hestia or Hera) can be channeled during housecleaning (Murphy-Hiscock, 2017: 45–49).

A sixth type of theurgy involves building theoretical models in your brain. To become more like the gods, Plato advocated contemplating the structure of our universe (*Timaeus*, 90b1-d7). By doing science, you can build a model of the universe inside your brain. Dawkins says that by building such a model in your brain, you get cognitively outside of the universe (1998: 312). But to stand outside of the universe in that way is to take a divine perspective on it, to more intensely instantiate the divine eidolon of our universe itself. Dawkins says this perspective induces “a feeling of awed wonder” which is “one of the highest experiences of which the human psyche is capable” (1998: *x*). He says it is a “deep aesthetic passion” (1998: *x*). Nietzsche said, “it is only as an aesthetic phenomenon that existence and the world are eternally justified" (*The Birth of Tragedy*, sec. 5). Dawkins continues by saying that the experience of this aesthetic ecstasy is "truly one of the things that makes life worth living" (1998: *x*). Our ability to take this divine perspective on our universe is "why it was worth coming to life in the first place" (1998: 313). For the Pagan, this scientific experience is religious ecstasy.

8 Conclusion

My goal here has been to do some analytic philosophy of contemporary Pagan religion. Analytic philosophy has developed an enormous system of conceptual tools which can be used to make sense out of religious doctrines and practices, and here I use these tools to try to clarify some of the metaphysical, theological, and ethical themes in contemporary Pagan religions. But much work remains to be done. For example, while my analytic work lays some foundations for arguments that justify many Pagan doctrines, I have not done much to construct those arguments. And there is much critical work to do as well: the tensions and problems in current Paganism need to be studied. I have barely even touched on Pagan practices, including the rich worlds of Pagan art and music.

My focus here has been fairly narrow: I have looked mainly at Paganisms which revive older indigenous Western religions. But contemporary Paganism is much broader than these particular revivals. It includes movements which take ideas and practices from many old indigenous Western traditions, as well as from Eastern traditions, and which fuse them into new religious and spiritual systems. To give just four examples: transformational festivals (such as Burning Man) continue to multiply and grow; many new religious naturalisms and eco-centric spiritualties are emerging; new forms of meditative and ritual practice are likewise growing in the West; there are new forms of religious pantheism and panpsychism. We are privileged to live in one of the greatest periods of religious change since the late Roman Empire. Religious creativity is flourishing in the West, and it will stimulate new philosophies and novel ways of life. Blessed be.

References

Aitamurto, K. & Simpson, S. (2014) *Modern Pagan and Native Faith Movements in Central and Eastern Europe*. New York: Routledge.

Alexander, T. (2007) *Hellenismos Today*. Raleigh, NC: Lulu.

Alexander, S. (2014) *The Modern Guide to Witchcraft*. New York: Simon & Schuster.

Andren, A. (2014) *Tracing Old Norse Cosmology*. Lund: Nordic Academic.

Arnhart, L. (1998) *Darwinian Natural Right: The Biological Ethics of Human Nature*. Albany, NY: SUNY.

Averill, E. & Gottlieb, J. (2021) The possible worlds theory of visual experience. *Inquiry*. https://doi.org/10.1080/0020174X.2021.1968946.

Axelrod, R. (1984) *The Evolution of Cooperation*. New York: Basic Books.

Balaguer, M. (1998) *Platonism and Anti-Platonism in Mathematics*. New York: Oxford.

Batty, M. (2023) *Teaching Witchcraft*. Woodbury, MN: Llewellyn.

Bauer, W. (2016) Physical intentionality, extrinsicness, and the direction of causation. *Acta Analytica 31*, 397–417. https://doi.org/10.1007/s12136-016-0283-2.

Bauer, W. (2022) *Causal Powers and the Intentionality Continuum*. New York: Cambridge.

Beckett, J. (2016) The otherworld is bleeding through. www.patheos.com/blogs/johnbeckett/2016/06/the-otherworld-is-bleeding-through.html.

Beckett, J. (2017) *The Path of Paganism*. Woodbury, MN: Llewellyn.

Beckett, J. (2019) *Paganism in Depth*. Woodbury, MN: Llewellyn.

Bekoff, M. & Pierce, J. (2009) *Wild Justice: The Moral Lives of Animals*. Chicago, IL: University of Chicago.

Belnap, N. (1992) Branching space-time. *Synthese 92*, 385–434.

Belnap, N. (2005) Branching histories approach to indeterminism and free will. In B. Brown & F. Lepage (eds.), *Truth and Probability: Essays in Honour of Hugues Leblanc*. London: College, 197–211.

Ben-Yami, H. (2007) The impossibility of backwards causation. *The Philosophical Quarterly 57* (228), 439–455. https://doi.org/10.1111/j.1467-9213.2007.494.x.

Bernabe, A. (2020) The primordial water: Between myth and philosophy. In A. Rengakos, P. Finglass, and B. Zimmerman (eds.), *More than Homer Knew*. Boston, MA: de Gruyter, 417–437. https://doi.org/10.1515/9783110695823.

Billington, P. (2011) *The Path of Druidry: Walking the Ancient Green Way*. Woodbury, MN: Llewellyn.

Bostrom, N. (2003) Are you living in a computer simulation? *Philosophical Quarterly 53* (211), 243–255. https://doi.org/10.1111/1467-9213.00309.

Boucherie, P., Loretto, M., Massen, J., and Bugnyar, T. (2019) What constitutes "social complexity" and "social intelligence" in birds? Lessons from ravens. *Behavioral Ecology and Sociobiology 73* (12), 1–14. https://doi.org/10.1007/s00265-018-2607-2.

Boyce, M. (2018) Wolves for Yellowstone: Dynamics in time and space. *Journal of Mammalogy 99* (5), 1021–1031. https://doi.org/10.1093/jmammal/gyy115.

Brymer, E. & Gray, T. (2009) Dancing with nature: Rhythm and harmony in extreme sport participation. *Journal of Adventure Education and Outdoor Learning 9* (2), 135–149. https://doi.org/10.1080/14729670903116912.

Buckland, R. (1986) *Complete Book of Witch Craft*. Woodbury, MN: Llewellyn.

Butler, E. (2014) *Essays on a Polytheistic Philosophy of Religion*. New York: Phaidra Editions.

Byghan, Y. (2018) *Modern Druidism: An Introduction*. Jefferson, NC: McFarland.

Cantrell, G. (2001) *Wiccan Beliefs and Practices*. Woodbury, MN: Llewellyn.

Carr-Gomm, P. (2006) *What Do Druids Believe?* London: Granta.

Carruthers, P. (2015) *The Centered Mind: What the Science of Working Memory Shows Us about the Nature of Human Thought*. New York: Oxford.

Cartwright, N. (1999) *The Dappled World*. New York: Cambridge.

Chalmers, D. (2022) *Reality+: Virtual Worlds and the Problems of Philosophy*. New York: W. W. Norton.

Chamberlain, L. (2016) *Wicca Book of Spells*. No city: Chamberlain.

Christensen, W. (2012) Natural sources of normativity. *Studies in History and Philosophy of Biological and Biomedical Sciences 43*, 104–112. https://doi.org/10.1016/j.shpsc.2011.05.009.

Christensen, W. & Bickhard, M. (2002) The process dynamics of normative function. *The Monist 85* (1), 3–28.

Clayton, N. & Emery, N. (2007) The social life of corvids. *Current Biology 17* (16), R652–R656.

Cozza, M., Ellison, K., & Katz, S. (2022) Hacking age. *Sociology Compass 16*, 1–12, e13034. https://doi.org/10.1111/soc4.13034.

Crowley, A. (1929) *Magick in Theory and Practice*. Paris: Lecram.

Crowley, V. (2001) *Way of Wicca*. London: Thorsons.

Crowley, V. (2003) *Wicca: A Comprehensive Guide*. New York: HarperCollins.

Csikszentmihalyi, M. (2002) *Flow: The Psychology of Optimal Experience*. New York: Harper & Row.

Cuhulain, K. (2011) *Pagan Religions*. Portland, OR: Acorn Guild.

Cunningham, S. (2004) *Wicca: A Guide for the Solitary Practitioner*. Woodbury, MN: Llewellyn.

Danielson, D., Satishchandran, G., & Wald, R. (2022) Black holes decohere quantum superpositions. *International Journal of Modern Physics D 31* (4), 1–16, 2241003. https://doi.org/10.1142/S0218271822410036.

Davy, B. (2007) *Introduction to Pagan Studies*. Lanham, MD: Altamira.

Dawkins, R. (1998) *Unweaving the Rainbow*. New York: Houghton Mifflin.

DeConick, A. (2020) The one god is no simple matter. In M. Novenson (ed.), *Monotheism and Christology in Greco-Roman Antiquity*. Boston, MA: Brill, 263–292. https://doi.org/10.1163/9789004438088_013.

Dennett, D. (2009) Darwin's "strange inversion of reasoning." *PNAS 106* (Supp. 1), 10061–10065. https://doi.org/10.1073/pnas.0904433106.

Dipert, R. (1997) The mathematical structure of the world: The world as graph. *Journal of Philosophy 94* (7), 329–358. https://doi.org/10.2307/2564553.

Dowe, P. (1997) A defense of backwards in time causation models in quantum mechanics. *Synthese 112* (2), 233–246. https://doi.org/10.1023/A:1004932911141.

Dreyfus, H. & Kelly, S. (2011) *All Things Shining: Reading the Western Classics to Find Meaning in a Secular Age*. New York: Free Press.

Driscoll, C. & Atwood, D. (2020) Mountaineering religion – a critical introduction. *Culture and Religion 21* (1), 1–17. https://doi.org/10.1080/14755610.2020.1858543.

Duerr, P. & Calosi, C. (2021) The general-relativistic case for super-substantivalism. *Synthese 199*, 13789–13822. https://doi.org/10.1007/s11229-021-03398-9.

Dummett, M. (1964) Bringing about the past. *The Philosophical Review 73* (3), 338–359. https://doi.org/10.2307/2183661.

Elder, Silver (2011) *Wiccan Celebrations*. Winchester: Moon Books.

Ellis, B. (2014) *The Philosophy of Nature: A Guide to the New Essentialism*. New York: Routledge. https://doi.org/10.4324/9781315710624.

Evans, P. (2015) Retrocausality at no extra cost. *Synthese 192* (4), 1139–1155. https://doi.org/10.1007/s11229-014-0605-0.

Farr, M. (2012) On A- and B-theoretic elements of branching spacetimes. *Synthese 188*, 85–116.

Farrar, J. & Farrar, S. (1981) *A Witches Bible*. Blaine, WA: Phoenix.

Fiala, A. (2008) Creation myths of the ancient world. In B. Taylor (ed.), *Encyclopedia of Religion and Nature*. New York: Bloomsbury, 431–433.

Filler, J. (2019) Relationality as the ground of being: The one as pure relation in Plotinus. *The International Journal of the Platonic Tradition 13* (1), 1–23. https://doi.org/10.1163/18725473-12341421.

Fitzpatrick, S. (2020) Chimpanzee normativity: Evidence and objections. *Biology & Philosophy 35* (45), 1–28. https://doi.org/10.1007/s10539-020-09763-1.

Flegel, P. (2018) Does Western philosophy have Egyptian roots? *Philosophy Now 128*, 28–31.

Franklin, J. (2015) Uninstantiated properties and semi-Platonist Aristotelianism. *Review of Metaphysics 69* (1), 25–45.

Gardner, G. (1954/2004) *Witchcraft Today*. New York: Kensington.

Gardner, G. (1959/2022) *The Meaning of Witchcraft*. Newburyport, MA: Weiser.

Greer, J. (2019) The One and the many: An essay on Pagan Neoplatonism. In M. Hardy (ed.), *Ascendant: Modern Essays on Polytheism and Theology*. No city: Bibliotheca Alexandria, 41–62.

Greer, J. (2021) *The Druid Path*. New York: Sterling.

Greer, J. (2023) *A World Full of Gods*. Lewes: Aeon.

Hanegraaff, W. (1996) *New Age Religion and Western Culture*. New York: Brill.

Harari, Y. (2015) *Homo Deus: A Brief History of Tomorrow*. New York: Vintage.

Hartshorne, C. (1965) *Anselm's Discovery: A Re-Examination of the Ontological Argument for God's Existence*. LaSalle, IL: Open Court.

Harvey, G. (2006) *Animism: Respecting the Living World*. New York: Columbia.

Hedenborg-White, M. (2014) Contemporary paganism. In J. Lewis & J. Petersen (eds.), *Controversial New Religions*. New York: Oxford, 315–331.

Hedreen, G. (2021) On the magnitude of the gods in materialist theology and Greek art. *Journal of Hellenic Studies 141*, 31–53. https://doi.org/10.1017/S0075426921000021.

Heidegger, M. (1929/1998) What is metaphysics? In W. McNeill (ed.), *Pathmarks*. New York: Cambridge, 82–96.

Hill, J. (2020) "I am the Gracious Goddess," Wiccan analytic theology. *Analytic Theology 8*, 152–177. https://doi.org/10.12978/jat.2020-8.091413070811.

Holldobler, B. & Wilson, E. O. (2009) *The Super-Organism: The Beauty, Elegance, and Strangeness of Insect Societies*. New York: W. W. Norton.

Horak, P. (2020) Who is, and who is not a pagan? *The Pomegranate 22* (2), 125–145.

Hutton, R. (2019) *The Triumph of the Moon: A History of Modern Pagan Witchcraft*. New York: Oxford.

Jamison, I. (2011) *Embodied Ethics and Contemporary Paganism*. PhD thesis. Milton Keynes: The Open University.

Joyce, R. (2006) *The Evolution of Morality*. Cambridge, MA: MIT.

Kadmus (2018) *True to the Earth: Pagan Political Theology*. Olympia, WA: Gods & Radicals Press.

Kang, M. (2011) *Sublime Dreams of Living Machines*. Cambridge, MA: Harvard.

Kardec, A. (1857) *The Spirits' Book*. Miami, FL: Edicei of America.

Ketcham, C. (2020) *Flowers and Honeybees: A Study of Morality in Nature*. Boston, MA: Brill Rodopi.

Kiers, T. & Denison, R. (2008) Sanctions, cooperation, and the stability of plant-rhizosphere mutualisms. *Annual Review of Ecology, Evolution, and Systematics 39*, 215–236. https://doi.org/10.1146/annurev.ecolsys.39.110707.173423.

Ladyman, J. (2023) Structural realism. In E. Zalta & U. Nodelman (eds.), *The Stanford Encyclopedia of Philosophy.* Stanford, CA: Stanford University. https://plato.stanford.edu/archives/sum2023/entries/structural-realism/.

Lafayllve, P. (2013) *A Practical Heathen's Guide to Asatru.* Woodbury, MN: Llewellyn.

Langer, E. (1975) The illusion of control. *Journal of Personality and Social Psychology 32* (2), 311–328.

Larrington, C. (trans.) (2014) *The Poetic Edda.* New York: Oxford.

Larvor, B. (2020) Weber and Coyote: Polytheism as a practical attitude. *Sophia 59*, 211–228. https://doi.org/10.1007/s11841-018-0641-1.

Laycock, J. (2012) "We are spirits of another sort": Ontological rebellion and religious dimensions of the Otherkin community. *Nova Religion 15* (3), 65–90. https://doi.org/10.1525/nr.2012.15.3.65.

Lehmkuhl, D. (2018) The metaphysics of super-substantivalism. *Nous 52* (1), 24–46. https://doi.org/10.1111/nous.12163.

Leigh, E. (2010) The evolution of mutualism. *Journal of Evolutionary Biology 23*, 2507–2528. https://doi.org/10.1111/j.1420-9101.2010.02114.x.

Leopold, A. (1949) *A Sand County Almanac.* New York: Oxford.

Lewis, D. (1978) Truth in fiction. *American Philosophical Quarterly 15*, 37–46.

Lewis, D. (1983) Individuation by acquaintance and by stipulation. *The Philosophical Review 92* (1), 3–32. https://doi.org/10.2307/2184519.

Lewis, D. (1986) *On the Plurality of Worlds.* Cambridge, MA: Blackwell.

Lewis, D. (2020) *Philosophical Letters of David Lewis Vol. 1.* Ed. H. Beebee & A. Fisher. New York: Oxford.

Li, S. & Purugganan, M. (2011) *Dictyostelium* as a model for social evolution. *Trends in Genetics 27* (2), 48–54. https://doi.org/10.1016/j.tig.2010.11.003.

Libby, E. & Ratcliff, W. (2014) Ratcheting the evolution of multicellularity. *Science 346* (6208), 426–427. https://doi.org/10.1126/science.12620.

Lupa (2021) *Nature Spirituality from the Ground Up.* No city: Self-published.

Lyng, S. (1990) Edgework: A social psychological analysis of voluntary risk taking. *American Journal of Sociology 95* (4), 851–886.

Mackie, J. L. (1966) The direction of causation. *The Philosophical Review 75* (4), 441–466. https://doi.org/10.2307/2183223.

MacLennan, B. (2013) *The Wisdom of Hypatia.* Woodbury, MN: Llewellyn.

Marwaha, S. & May, E. (2016) Precognition: The only form of psi? *Journal of Consciousness Studies 23* (3–4), 76–100.

Meredith, J. (2013) *Rituals of Celebration: Honoring the Seasons of Life through the Wheel of the Year*. Woodbury, MN: Llewellyn.

Mills, S. & Cote, I. (2010) Crime and punishment in a roaming cleanerfish. *Proceedings of the Royal Society B 277*, 3617–3622. https://doi.org/10.1098/rspb.2010.0941.

Molnar, G. (2006) *Powers: A Study in Metaphysics*. Edited by S. Mumford. New York: Oxford.

Moreno, A. & Mossio, M. (2015) *Biological Autonomy*. New York: Springer.

Moye, J. (2021) How studying witchcraft changed my relationship with the outdoors. *Outside Magazine* (31 October). www.outsideonline.com/outdoor-adventure/snow-sports/witch-witchcraft-wicca-nature/.

Muller, T. (2012) Branching in the landscape of possibilities. *Synthese 188*, 41–65.

Mumford, S. & Anjum, R. (2011) *Getting Causes from Powers*. New York: Oxford.

Murphy-Hiscock, A. (2017) *The Green Witch*. New York: Simon & Schuster.

Myers, B. (2013) *The Earth, the Gods, and the Soul: A History of Pagan Philosophy, from the Iron Age to the Twenty-First Century*. Winchester, KY: Moon Books.

Noe, A. (2018) Art and entanglement in *Strange Tools*. *Phenomenology and Mind 14*, 30–36.

Nordvig, M. (2020) *Asatru for Beginners*. Emeryville, CA: Rockridge.

O'Donoghue, S. (2022) *Courting the Wild Queen*. Luxemburg: Ritona Press.

Oliver, A. & Smiley, T. (2013) Zilch. *Analysis 73* (4), 601–613. https://doi.org/10.1093/analys/ant074.

Opsopaus, J. (2022) *The Secret Texts of Hellenic Polytheism*. Woodbury, MN: Llewellyn.

Orr, E. (2011) *The Wakeful World: Animism, Mind and the Self in Nature*. Hants: John Hunt.

Osborne, R. (2010) Relics and remains in an ancient Greek world full of anthropomorphic gods. *Past and Present 206* (Supp. 5), 56–72. https://doi.org/10.1093/pastj/gtq012.

Ostrowski, E. (2019) Enforcing cooperation in the social amoebae. *Current Biology 29*, R474–R484. https://doi.org/10.1016/j.cub.2019.04.022.

Palmqvist, C.-J. (2023) The old gods as a live possibility: On the rational feasibility of non-doxastic paganism. *Religious Studies* 59, 651–644. https://doi.org/10.1017/S003441252200049X.

Parsons, K. (2022) Reviving pagan spirituality: A manifesto. *Religions 13*, 942, 1–11. https://doi.org/10.3390/rel13100942.

Paxson, A. (2021) *Essential Asatru*. New York: Kensington.

Peirce, C. S. (1965) *Collected Papers of Charles Sanders Peirce*. Edited by C. Hartshorne & P. Weiss. Cambridge, MA: Harvard.

Pierce, J. & Bekoff, M. (2012) Wild justice redux: What we know about social justice in animals and why it matters. *Social Justice Research 25*, 122–139. https://doi.org/10.1007/s11211-012-0154-y.

Pigliucci, M. (2017) *How to Be a Stoic: Using Ancient Philosophy to Live a Modern Life*. New York: Basic Books.

Pizza, M. & Lewis, J. (eds.) (2009) *Handbook of Contemporary Paganism*. Boston, MA: Brill.

Placek, T. (2012) On individuals in branching histories. *Synthese 188*, 23–39.

Plebuch, D. (2010) *Heidegger's Fourfold*. PhD thesis. University of Illinois at Urbana-Champaign.

Priest, G. (2001) Heidegger and the grammar of being. In R. Gaskin (ed.), *Grammar in Early Twentieth-Century Philosophy*. New York: Routledge, 238–252.

Priest, G. (2014) *One*. New York: Oxford.

Ramstedt, M. (2007) Metaphor or invocation? The convergence between modern paganism and fantasy fiction. *Journal of Ritual Studies 21* (1), 1–15.

Redfield, A. (2017) An analysis of the experiences and integration of transpersonal phenomena induced by electronic dance music events. *International Journal of Transpersonal Studies 36* (1), 67–80. https://doi.org/10.24972/ijts.2017.36.1.67.

Redick, K. (2018) Interpreting contemporary pilgrimage as spiritual journey or aesthetic tourism along the Appalachian trail. *International Journal of Religious Tourism and Pilgrimage 6* (2), 78–88, Article 10.

Roderick, T. (2005) *Wicca: A Year and a Day*. Woodbury, MI: Llewellyn.

Rodgers, J. (2020) A modern polytheism? Nietzsche and James. *Journal of Speculative Philosophy 34* (1), 69–96. https://doi.org/10.5325/jspecphil.34.1.0069.

Rogerson, J. (2003) What is holiness? In S. Barton (ed.), *Holiness: Past and Present*. New York: Continuum, 3–21.

Rountree, K. (2002) How magic works: New Zealand feminist witches theories of ritual action. *Anthropology of Consciousness 13* (1), 42–59. https://doi.org/10.1525/ac.2002.13.1.42.

Rountree, K. (2010) *Crafting Contemporary Pagan Identities in a Catholic Society*. Farnham: Ashgate.

Rountree, K. (ed.) (2015) *Contemporary Pagan and Native Faith Movements in Europe*. New York: Berghahn.

Rowlands, M. (2012) *Can Animals Be Moral?* New York: Oxford.

Ruickbie, L. (2004) *Witchcraft out of the Shadows: A Complete History*. London: Robert Hale.

Sabin, T. (2011) *Wicca for Beginners*. Woodbury, MI: Llewellyn.

Schnurbein, S. (2016) *Norse Revival: Transformations of Germanic Neopaganism*. Leiden: Brill.

Scriven, M. (1956) Randomness and the causal order. *Analysis 17* (1), 5–9. https://doi.org/10.2307/3326756.

Sebastiani, A. (2020) *Paganism for Beginners*. Emeryville, CA: Rockridge Press.

Shaw, G. (2013) Theurgy. In R. Bagnall, K. Brodersen, C. Champion, A. Erskine, and S. Huebner (eds.) *The Encyclopedia of Ancient History*. New York: Blackwell, 6714–6715.

Shaw, G. (2014) *Theurgy and the Soul: The Neoplatonism of Iamblichus*. 2nd ed. Kettering, OH: Angelico Press.

Shaw, G. (2015) Taking the shape of the gods: A theurgic reading of Hermetic rebirth. *Aries –Journal for the Study of Western Esotericism 15*, 136–169. https://doi.org/10.1163/15700593-01501009.

Smith, R. (2019) *The Way of Fire and Ice: The Living Tradition of Norse Paganism*. Woodbury, MN: Llewellyn.

Sonnex, C., Roe, C., & Roxburgh, E. (2022) Flow, liminality, and eudaimonia: Pagan ritual practice as a gateway to a life with meaning. *Journal of Humanistic Psychology 62* (2), 233–256. https://doi.org/10.1177/0022167820927577.

Squire, L. (2021) *The Witch of the Forest's Guide to Natural Magick*. London: Quarto Group.

Starhawk. (1999) *The Spiral Dance*. New York: HarperCollins.

Stein, D. (1990) *Casting the Circle*. Freedom, CA: The Crossing Press.

Steinhart, E. (2014) *Your Digital Afterlives: Computational Theories of Life after Death*. New York: Palgrave Macmillan.

Steinhart, E. (2016) Eupraxia as a religion of nature. *American Journal of Theology and Philosophy 37* (3), 227–245.

Steinhart, E. (2018) Spirit. *Sophia 56* (4), 557–571. https://doi.org/10.1007/s11841-017-0573-1.

Steinhart, E. (2020a) *Believing in Dawkins: The New Spiritual Atheism*. New York: Palgrave Macmillan.

Steinhart, E. (2020b) Theurgy and transhumanism. *Archai 29*, 1–23, e02905. https://doi.org/10.14195/1984-249X_29_5.

Steinhart, E. (2022) *Atheistic Platonism: A Manifesto*. New York: Palgrave Macmillan.

Steinhart, E. (2023) Atheistic modal realism. *Religious Studies 59* (4), 700–713. https://doi.org/10.1017/S0034412522000609.

Strmiska, M. (2020) Arguing with the ancestors: Making the case for a paganism without racism. In H. Emore & J. Leader (eds.), *Paganism and Its Discontents:*

Enduring Problems of Racialized Identity. Newcastle: Cambridge Scholars, 1–21.

Stutfield, H. (1918) Mountaineering as a religion. *The Alpine Journal 32* (217–219), 241–247.

Sylvan, R. (2005) *Trance Formation*. New York: Routledge.

Sylvan, D. (2012) *The Circle Within*. Woodbury, MI: Llewellyn.

Taggart, D. (2019) Do Thor and Odin have bodies? Superperception and divine intervention among the Old Norse gods. *Religions 10*, 486, 1–21. https://doi.org/10.3390/rel10080468.

Taylor, B. (2007) Surfing into spirituality and a new, aquatic nature religion. *Journal of the American Academy of Religion 75* (4), 923–951. https://doi.org/10.1093/jaarel/lfm067.

Tillich, P. (1951) *Systematic Theology.* Vol. 1. Chicago, IL: University of Chicago.

Tillich, P. (1952) *The Courage to Be*. New Haven, CT: Yale.

Tillich, P. (1957) *Systematic Theology.* Vol. 2. Chicago, IL: University of Chicago.

Tomasello, M. (2016) *A Natural History of Human Morality.* Cambridge, MA: Harvard.

Travers, M. (2018) Trees, rivers, and gods: Paganism in the work of Martin Heidegger. *Journal of European Studies 48* (2), 133–143. https://doi.org/10.1177/0047244118767820.

Tugby, M. (2022) *Putting Properties First: A Platonic Metaphysics for Natural Modality.* New York: Oxford.

Van Dijk, J. (1995) Myth and mythmaking in ancient Egypt. *Civilizations of the Ancient Near East 3*, 1697–1709.

Vanderbeck, P. (2020) *Green Witchcraft*. Emeryville, CA: Rockridge.

Vanhala, J. (2014) How to approach Heideggerian gods. *Analecta Husserliana 116*, 369–380. https://doi.org/10.1007/978-3-319-02015-0_26.

Vincent, S., Ring, R., & Andrews, K. (2019) Normative practices of other animals. In A. Zimmerman (ed.), *The Routledge Handbook of Moral Epistemology.* New York: Routledge, 57–83.

Watson, G. (2008) *A Witch's Natural History.* London: Troy.

Wen, X.-G. (2018) Four revolutions in physics and the second quantum revolution – A unification of force and matter by quantum information. *International Journal of Modern Physics B 32* (26), 1–21, 1830010. https://doi.org/10.1142/S0217979218300104.

White, E. (2015) *Wicca: History, Belief, and Community in Modern Pagan Witchcraft*. Eastbourne: Sussex Academic Press.

Wildermuth, R. (2021) *Being Pagan*. Luxembourg: Ritona.

Williams, B. (2016) *For the Love of the Gods*. Woodbury, MN: Llewellyn.
Wronski, L. & Placek, T. (2009) On Minkowskian branching structures. *Studies in History and Philosophy of Modern Physics 40*, 251–258.
York, M. (2003) *Pagan Theology*. New York: New York University.
York, M. (2015) *Pagan Ethics*. New York: Springer.

Acknowledgments

I would like to thank Yujin Nagasawa for inviting me to write this Element. I am grateful for many conversations about these topics with Stephanie Rivera Berruz, Andrei Buckareff, Tom Clark, Helen de Cruz, Dan Fincke, Pete Mandik, Yujin Nagasawa, Graham Oppy, Kevin Schilbrack, Joe Schmidt, Daniel Strain, Michael Lee Sudduth, Ben Vilhauer, and many others. Thanks are due as well to Dean Zimmerman and the Rutgers Philosophy of Religion Center. I thank John Beckett and Mark Green for reading an earlier draft. I am greatly indebted to Carl-Johan Palmqvist for providing many helpful comments on an earlier draft. Special thanks are due to an anonymous reviewer for providing extremely insightful and productive comments.

Cambridge Elements

Global Philosophy of Religion

Yujin Nagasawa
University of Oklahoma

Yujin Nagasawa is Kingfisher College Chair of the Philosophy of Religion and Ethics and Professor of Philosophy at the University of Oklahoma. He is the author of *The Problem of Evil for Atheists* (2024), *Maximal God: A New Defence of Perfect Being Theism* (2018), *Miracles: A Very Short Introduction* (2018), *The Existence of God: A Philosophical Introduction* (2011), and *God and Phenomenal Consciousness* (2008), along with numerous articles. He is the editor-in-chief of *Religious Studies* and served as the president of the British Society for the Philosophy of Religion from 2017 to 2019.

About the Series

This Cambridge Elements series provides concise and structured overviews of a wide range of religious beliefs and practices, with an emphasis on global, multi-faith viewpoints. Leading scholars from diverse cultural backgrounds and geographical regions explore topics and issues that have been overlooked by Western philosophy of religion.

Cambridge Elements

Global Philosophy of Religion

Elements in the Series

Afro-Brazilian Religions
José Eduardo Porcher

The African Mood Perspective on God and the Problem of Evil
Ada Agada

Contemporary Pagan Philosophy
Eric Steinhart

A full series listing is available at: www.cambridge.org/EGPR

For EU product safety concerns, contact us at Calle de José Abascal, 56–1°, 28003 Madrid, Spain or eugpsr@cambridge.org.

www.ingramcontent.com/pod-product-compliance
Ingram Content Group UK Ltd.
Pitfield, Milton Keynes, MK11 3LW, UK
UKHW022143080726
473066UK00010B/737

* 9 7 8 1 0 0 9 4 5 2 3 8 0 *